MAKE IT HAPPEN!

Unbeatable Bible Principles To Help You Achieve More In Life

Emmanuel Idu

Copyright © 2015 Emmanuel Idu
All rights reserved. No part of this book may be reproduced or transmitted in any form or by any means, electronically, mechanically, or otherwise, without the written permission of the author.

Unless otherwise indicated, all Bible passages are from the 1769 King James Version of the Holy Bible (also known as the Authorized Version).

ISBN-10: 94-92018-04-5
ISBN-13: 978-94-92018-04-5

Published by

Emmanuel Idu
INTERNATIONAL

EmmanuelIdu.org

Dedication

To all progress-loving people around the world

Acknowledgment

With gratitude to God for His continued inspirations from the Bible; to my precious wife, Irene, and to our daughters, Caroline and Darielle, for allowing me the time to write; and to our churches, friends, and ministry partners around the world for their continued prayerful support

Emmanuel Idu

TABLE OF CONTENT

DEDICATION III
ACKNOWLEDGMENT IV
TABLE OF CONTENT V
PREFACE VI
1. THE ILLUSION WE CALL "IDEAL" 8
2. OVERCOMING PERSONAL INSECURITIES 26
3. VICTORY SECRETS OF QUEEN ESTHER 37
4. HOW TO QUALIFY FOR YOUR NEXT LEVEL......... 64
5. FIGHTERS ACHIEVE MORE IN LIFE! 87
6. MAKE IT HAPPEN! 113
7. ARISE AND SHINE! 146
ABOUT THE AUTHOR 188

Preface

Yes, the Good Shepherd leads His flock through the valley of the shadow of death and prepares a table in the presence of the enemy.

It takes confidence and faith to keep walking with the Good Shepherd when death lurks in the shadows, and it takes absolute confidence to enjoy a meal with enemies all around.

Such situations are not the ideals that most people long for, but they are parts of the realities of the life of progress with God.

With God, the true ideal is not the absence of challenges in your life, but the presence of God in your challenging situations. We face storms even when we have the Lord Jesus in the boat! Therefore, you must be strong in your faith and face your challenges with confidence, by God's grace.

God can supply you with water in the desert and make a way for you through the wilderness. He can give you exceptional ideas and make you rich in a poor country. The true ideal is having God on your side. Do not accept any excuse that keeps you resigned to living a passive lifestyle.

Living the true ideal is living in partnership with God and following His principles and direction to make things happen, even in the toughest of times and in conditions that many would consider unfavorable.

Many situations that look unfavorable can actually turn out in our favor if we love God enough to follow His purpose and calling for our lives.

Many people settle for less in life because they allow adversities to discourage and intimidate them. You are to be different from such people. Decide to pursue the plan of God for your life with the determination to succeed, and He will help you along the way.

Embrace the plan of God, and make up your mind to make it happen!

1. THE ILLUSION WE CALL "IDEAL"

"He that observeth the wind shall not sow; and he that regardeth the clouds shall not reap" (Eccl. 11:4).

"I wish I had more money; I would have done more for orphans." "I wish I had more time; I would have read more books." "I wish I was younger; I would have gone back to school."

"I wish I was older; I would have started my own business." "I wish I had more political connections; I would have launched a new project."

"I wish more people believed in me; I would have seen more doors open for me to show my talents to the world." "I wish I was born in a different country; I would have achieved more in life."

"I wish I was born a man; I would have achieved greater goals." "I wish I was born a woman; I would have had an easier life."

Do these thoughts sound familiar to you? Have you ever been in a place where you felt that you were just missing one or two things necessary to have a major breakthrough? Do you have qualities and potentials that you are finding difficult to develop and deploy because you think that you are missing one or more significant elements?

If so, then you are not alone. Often, even the most faithful and dedicated people in churches feel the same way.

Our opening Bible passage tells us that those who allow temporary external indicators, forces, or circumstances to direct their actions will end up unfruitful and without harvest in life.

The Bible also reminds us that the righteous also go through challenges in this life:

"Many are the afflictions of the righteous: but the LORD delivereth him out of them all"
(Ps. 34:19).

In other words, one can do all of the right things and still face difficult situations in life. One can have good intentions and good plans and still attract opposition. It is possible to be in the will of God and still encounter challenges. Please understand that it is possible to have many people around you and still feel lonely. Life is tough, and one must toughen up to reach greater goals.

Many people around the world feel inadequate and watch many years of their lives waste away without pursuing their dreams because they feel that they need to wait for better times, more reliable people, and

Make it Happen!

better opportunities to come their way before taking action.

Such people usually have certain factors in mind that they feel must come together for them to progress and achieve success. These factors may be material, natural, human, circumstantial, legal, social, financial, political, geographical, climatic, or divine in nature.

They desire to have all of the right things in place so that they can feel comfortable and confident and believe that they will succeed. To them, having this combination of factors is the "ideal" place and condition to be in before taking steps towards success.

If, by some chance, they make efforts in the absence of such factors and fail, they will blame their failure on the missing factors. If they fail a few times, they will begin to think that they are failures, thus increasing their desire to see all factors in place from the onset before undertaking new ventures in the near future.

They then develop the unhealthy habit of procrastinating, postponing actions indefinitely as they continue to fantasize about the "perfect" day, time, person, or circumstance that would create the "ideal" setting for them to succeed. They will fear failure and try to stay "safe" by doing nothing!

In the meantime, as the fear of failure keeps them procrastinating and waiting for "ideal" circumstances or "perfect" scenarios, they will observe and see other people succeeding in life. This will lead them to assume that such people succeed in life, only because they are "lucky," "fortunate," or "blessed," and they will feel that such people succeed because of the absence of adversities.

They assume that great achievers have special advantages over other people, and that such advantages make life easier for them and make their successes a piece of cake. They assume that blessed people do not face serious obstacles. They consider their own challenges too heavy and feel disadvantaged and less fortunate in life, consequently making them indulge in self-pity.

To these "pitiful" people, life is full of unfair shortages, trials, temptations, obstacles, pitfalls, disappointments, betrayals, and so on, as they see themselves as victims on the receiving end of the negative experiences. They feel that they have worked for too long without seeing the fruits of their labor, and have made too many attempts to achieve goals without success.

Some of them give up and stop trying. Others expect support to come from the people in their lives and feel disappointed when their trusted friends, family members, and acquaintances fail to deliver the kind of help that they expect. They feel lonely and abandoned by people and soon develop a negative outlook regarding relationships. "No one is helping me!" They complain.

There are also those who turn to God for help through prayers and then fold their hands and sit back, refraining from making any personal efforts, and waiting for God to perform miracles, while God expects them to take the steps necessary for activating such miracles. They tend to "wait" for God at the same time that God is waiting for them!

Such people quote Bible passages out of context to support their passive approach to life and assume that whatever God wants to see succeed succeeds anyway. To them, failing in any venture confirms that the venture was not the will of God because, in their worldview, the will of God always happens—no matter what a person does or does not do.

They assume that God always provides the ideal situation whenever He wants projects to succeed. To them, experiencing opposition is a sure indication that a person is operating outside of the will of God.

As we saw in an earlier passage, the fact of the matter is that righteous people, living in the will of God, also go through challenges. They just do not stay down when they fall. They get up and move on. They refuse to surrender to difficult circumstances. They are tough in their minds and strong in their faith, and they simply choose to press forward, no matter what!

"For a just man falleth seven times, and riseth up again: but the wicked shall fall into mischief" (Prov. 24:16)

"Rejoice not against me, O mine enemy: when I fall, I shall arise; when I sit in darkness, the LORD shall be a light unto me" (Mic. 7:8).

The Lord Jesus Christ told His disciples that they would experience tribulations in this world, but He also assured them of peace in the midst of their challenges:

"These things I have spoken unto you, that in me ye might have peace. In the world ye shall have tribulation: but be of good cheer; I have overcome the world" (John 16:33).

We must remember that, when under the leadership of the Great Shepherd, the Lord Himself, we can even walk through the *valley of the shadow of death* surrounded by evil! The Lord can prepare a great table for us in the *presence of the enemy*!

Many people read in Psalm 23 about the Good Shepherd and pay attention to the pleasant phrases in the passage, while failing to notice the challenges associated with the comforting promises. Read the psalm carefully once more, and you will notice some interesting realities:

"The LORD is my shepherd; I shall not want. He maketh me to lie down in green pastures: he leadeth me beside the still waters. He restoreth my soul: he leadeth me in the paths of righteousness for his name's sake. Yea, though I walk through the valley of the shadow of death, I will fear no evil: for thou art with me; thy rod and thy staff they comfort me. Thou preparest a table before me in the presence of mine enemies: thou anointest my head with oil; my cup runneth over. Surely goodness and mercy shall follow me all the days of my life: and I will dwell in the house of the LORD for ever" (Ps. 23:1–6).

Yes, the Good Shepherd leads His flock through the valley of the shadow of death and prepares a table in the presence of the enemy. It takes confidence and faith to keep walking with the Good Shepherd when death lurks in the shadows, and it takes absolute

Make it Happen!

confidence to enjoy a meal with enemies all around. Such situations are not the ideals that most people long for, but they are part of the reality of the life of progress with God.

The disciples experienced storms even when they acted in obedience to the Lord Jesus, and the Master was with them in the boat when the storm came upon them in the passage below. Notice that crossing to the "other side" was the Lord's idea, not theirs. In reality, they experienced the storm after acting in obedience to the initiative and instruction of the Master!

"And the same day, when the even was come, he saith unto them, Let us pass over unto the other side. And when they had sent away the multitude, they took him even as he was in the ship. And there were also with him other little ships. And there arose a great storm of wind, and the waves beat into the ship, so that it was now full. And he was in the hinder part of the ship, asleep on a pillow: and they awake him, and say unto him, Master, carest thou not that we perish? And he arose, and rebuked the wind, and said unto the sea, Peace, be still. And the wind ceased, and there was a great calm. And he said unto them, Why are ye so fearful? how is it that ye have no faith? And they feared exceedingly, and said one to another, What manner of man is this, that even the wind and the sea obey him?" (Mark 4:35–41).

The disciples did the right thing by obeying the Master and following His instructions to cross to the other side, yet they experienced a storm! The Lord Jesus was with them in the boat, yet the trip felt rough, dangerous, and life threatening to them!

With God, the true ideal is not the absence of challenges in your life, but the presence of God in your challenging situations. We face storms even when we have the Lord Jesus in the boat! Therefore, you must be strong in faith and face your challenges with confidence, by God's grace.

"Ideal" is not normal!

The ideal that most people long for is not normal. On the contrary, it is completely unrealistic.

To have an ideal situation means to have the conditions that are most favorable for your goal in position at the right time, in the right place, with the right people, with the right weather, at the right costs, and so on.

It means to feel and know that you lack nothing that you consider essential for the successful realization of your dreams. It is having the greatest number of people in your life supporting your goals and making helpful contributions towards the fulfillment of your dreams.

It means coming to a place where you have all of the factors in place for you to reasonably guarantee success. It means having your mind, spirit, and body in the right order so that it will take a miracle for you to fail!

Think about it for a moment. How realistic is such a condition?

Make it Happen!

Having the "ideal" requires you to have the experience, inspiration, revelation, character, sentiment, emotions, psyche, spiritual condition, temperament, and many other variable factors line up properly in perfect proportion and in absolute harmony for each goal that you want to pursue.

In many cases, to have your ideal, the political situation needs to be right. The economic situation needs to be perfect. Heaven, Hell, and the world around you need to be in your favor at the same time!

How realistic is such a condition? Such a condition is not realistic!

The fact is that we do not normally have all of these perfect conditions and variables in place in real life.

Our "ideal" exists as the exception, not the norm. Ideal conditions, as most people desire them, are so remote that we cannot afford to wait for them before taking steps. Anyone waiting for such perfect conditions before they will do things will rarely take steps in life. Such a person lives in a fantasy, in a state of mind that we may rightly call an *illusion*.

What does it mean to live in an illusion?

Within our context, an illusion is something that people believe but that does not qualify as real or factual. It is a fantasy, a misconception, a kind of deception.

Many people live their lives in illusions. They expect things that are not proper to expect. They bury their heads in the sand and hope that their challenges will disappear. They have the habit of remaining passive in the hope that doing nothing will eventually change their realities and bring about ideal situations.

While some adversities may disappear with time, and waiting out certain situations may eventually turn things around, the habit of procrastinating as a way of life is often a characteristic associated with people living with illusions.

Such people often shy away from their responsibilities and expect other people to take steps on their behalf.

They feel that someone in their life owes them success on moral, natural, or legal grounds, and they look to their family members, friends, neighbors, employers, government, acquaintances, church members, and other people in their lives to deliver their success.

People living in illusion have the wrong picture of great achievers. In their minds, such achievers always had ideal situations, succeeded too easily or quickly, and did not need to go through tough challenges.

They think that achievers simply rode on the back of God and did not need to do anything on their own. They falsely assume that such people succeeded overnight and did not need to work smart, work hard, make any sacrifices, or go through serious pressures.

The fact of the matter is that most achievers progressed through tough times, working wisely and working hard in the midst of adversity. Many achievers walked through the valley of the shadow of death, ate on the table of the Lord in the presence of their enemies, labored day and night, experienced betrayals from trusted friends, survived with limited resources, went through many moments of discouragement, and prevailed in bad circumstances before reaching their goals.

Most great achievers did not have ideal situations. Many of them worked together with God to create their own ideals and make seemingly impossible things possible. They took responsibility for their own progress in the will of God and fought tough and long battles to make things happen before seeing lasting results.

Great achievers progress in the midst of adversities.

Paul the Apostle wrote:

"For a great door and effectual is opened unto me, and there are many adversaries" (1 Cor. 16:9).

Many Christians admire Paul the Apostle for his extraordinary achievements in spreading the Gospel during his own time, but only a relatively few of them actually take the time to study and realize the fact that he succeeded in the midst of many adversities. He did not live an easy life.

Most Bible students simply know that Paul had extraordinary results in Asia and touched cities with the Gospel of the Lord Jesus Christ. Unfortunately, their one-sided knowledge of him stops there. What many fail to understand is that Paul also had a tough time in Asia.

He wrote:

"For we would not, brethren, have you ignorant of our trouble which came to us in Asia, that we were pressed out of measure, above strength, insomuch that we despaired even of life: But we had the sentence of death in ourselves, that we should not trust in ourselves, but in God which raiseth the dead: Who delivered us from so great a death, and doth deliver: in whom we trust that he will yet deliver us" (2 Cor. 1:8–10).

Like many great achievers, Paul the Apostle pressed forward in the midst of adversities. His challenges only pulled him closer to God and increased his faith and his resolve to do the will of his Creator. He did not allow obstacles and adversities to hinder him from pursuing the purpose of God for his life.

Here are a few more Bible passages from Paul's life showing some of his challenges:

"We are troubled on every side, yet not distressed; we are perplexed, but not in despair; Persecuted, but not forsaken; cast down, but not destroyed; Always bearing about in the body the dying of the Lord Jesus, that the life also of Jesus might be made manifest in our body" (2 Cor. 4:8–10).

Make it Happen!

"For, when we were come into Macedonia, our flesh had no rest, but we were troubled on every side; without were fightings, within were fears" (2 Cor. 7:5).

"But in all things approving ourselves as the ministers of God, in much patience, in afflictions, in necessities, in distresses, In stripes, in imprisonments, in tumults, in labours, in watchings, in fastings; By pureness, by knowledge, by longsuffering, by kindness, by the Holy Ghost, by love unfeigned, By the word of truth, by the power of God, by the armour of righteousness on the right hand and on the left, By honour and dishonour, by evil report and good report: as deceivers, and yet true; As unknown, and yet well known; as dying, and, behold, we live; as chastened, and not killed; As sorrowful, yet always rejoicing; as poor, yet making many rich; as having nothing, and yet possessing all things" (2 Cor. 6:4–10).

After preaching the Gospel in many cities, Paul revisited Lystra, Iconium, and Antioch, encouraging the believers there to continue in the faith, and making it clear to them that they must press through tribulation in their determination to enter into the Kingdom of God. He wanted them to understand the importance of pressing forward in the midst of challenges.

"And when they had preached the gospel to that city, and had taught many, they returned again to Lystra, and to Iconium, and Antioch, Confirming the souls of the disciples, and exhorting them to continue in the faith, and that we must through much tribulation enter into the kingdom of God" (Acts 14:21–22).

David's Experience

Many people admire King David's success, but only a relatively few take the time to notice the challenges that he went through. His life was far from easy, and his situations were often far from ideal, at least from the human and natural standpoint.

David's life defied many odds. As the youngest son, he was not a significant member of his family, yet God anointed David to be king. David then served King Saul faithfully, risking his own life for the land, yet King Saul tried to kill him several times.

David was homeless, hungry, accused falsely, hunted by a reigning king, isolated from his family members, and suspected of treason. How ideal was that? He was busy doing his best, but his reality was far from pleasant. God chose and anointed him to reign, but his life only appeared to be deteriorating. His ordeal included sleeping in a cave in the mountains and roaming around from coast to coast as a refugee.

In the midst of his own challenges, he had to take care of other people and be a captain of troublemakers.

"David therefore departed thence, and escaped to the cave Adullam: and when his brethren and all his father's house heard it, they went down thither to him. And every one that was in distress, and every one that was in debt, and every one that was discontented, gathered themselves unto him; and he became a captain over them: and there were with him about four hundred men" (1 Sam. 22:1-2).

He had no income in the wilderness, yet his men looked to him to feed them. He had to behave himself, teach his men godly principles, respect God's order and the life of King Saul, and continue to trust God even when his own life was in danger.

David's situation was far from ideal, yet he held on to the will of God, pressed forward in the plan of God, and became the greatest king in the land!

Looking back at his experience, David could not help but testify about God's faithfulness:

"For thou art my lamp, O LORD: and the LORD will lighten my darkness. For by thee I have run through a troop: by my God have I leaped over a wall" (2 Sam. 22:29-30).

David ran through the troop and leaped over a wall with God's help. David did it—with God.

God has things for you to do with His help. The situations may not be ideal, but with God on your side, you can choose to move forward.

Create your own true ideal with God!

The only true ideal is living in partnership with God and following His principles and direction to make things happen, even in the toughest of times and in conditions that many would consider unfavorable. Many situations that look unfavorable can actually turn out in our favor if we love God enough to follow His purpose and calling for our lives.

"And we know that all things work together for good to them that love God, to them who are the called according to his purpose" (Rom. 8:28).

If something is the will of God for your life, and you know that He wants you to accomplish it, then it becomes your responsibility to discover the principles and conditions necessary for the fulfillment of that purpose and to do everything possible to make it happen.

If your situation is not "ideal," then recreate the situation. If things look impossible, trust God and find ways to make them possible.

If the people around you do not support you, then get other people who will support you. If you cannot find them in your current environment, then do your research and ask God for permission to go and find them wherever they exist on the earth.

If you are a child of God, then you know that the entire world belongs to your Heavenly Father! Remember that man created the natural boundaries that we know today. You did not choose your place of birth, but you can work with God to choose where you live once you have the maturity to make such a decision.

If you must move, then do your research. Find out the qualifications for obtaining visas and securing resident permits, and then qualify yourself to move. If God does not want you to move, then He has seen possibilities for your progress in the place where you are. Do not allow anything that you see or feel to the contrary to discourage you.

God can supply you with water in the desert and make a way for you through the wilderness. He can give you exceptional ideas and make you rich in a poor country. Having God on your side is the true ideal.

Work towards God's goals for your life. If you need to study more, then study. If you need to make more money, make the money. If you do not know how to make money, learn from someone who knows how to make money. Pay that person gladly if necessary. If you have no money to pay someone to teach you how to make money, then negotiate and offer one or more services in return.

Do not accept any excuse that keeps you resigned to a passive lifestyle.

If you need to build strategic relationships, then invest your resources and build strategic relationships.

If God's spouse for you is not in your environment, then go where such a spouse is, or bring your future spouse to your location. Unless God shows you otherwise, your spouse does not have to come from your place of birth or current residence, and does not even have to have your skin color.

Learn to be flexible and adaptable, and you will see opportunities that you never thought existed.

If you are a child of God, then the world is your territory, and your Heavenly Father owns the universe.

Do not limit your options where God has not placed a limit on you. Learn to work with God in creating and recreating your own ideal.

Do not just wait for something to happen. Make things happen with the abilities of God in you. Opposition is normal. Challenges are normal. Ideal situations are rare! Learn to prosper in the midst of adversities, and you will have no shortage of opportunities.

Many people settle for less in life because they allow adversity to discourage and intimidate them. You are to be different from such people. Decide to pursue the plan of God for your life with the determination to succeed, and He will help you along the way.

God created you and left you in this world for a purpose. God intended you to be His gift to your generation. Make up your mind to live up to His expectations. Embrace His great plans and dreams, and work with Him to make them happen!

In the next chapter, we shall see how to overcome the menace of personal insecurity.

2. OVERCOMING PERSONAL INSECURITIES

"And there we saw the giants, the sons of Anak, which come of the giants: and we were in our own sight as grasshoppers, and so we were in their sight" (Num. 13:33).

The passage above is a portion of the report presented by the majority of the spies of Israel after their visit to the land that they intended to take. They reported positively about the fruitfulness of the land but felt insecure about their ability to actually defeat the inhabitants there and take the land. They were insecure because they saw great giants in the land and felt like grasshoppers—too little and too weak to fight such notorious giants.

They loved the land, but ten of the twelve spies concluded that they were not capable of taking it. Insecurity was a hindrance to them, and those ten spies never made it into the Promised Land. They focused too much on the strength of the enemy and too little on the power of God.

Many challenges in life can appear insurmountable if we forget the power of God and His desire to work in us, with us, and through us to accomplish His goals.

It is natural for people to feel insecure and inadequate. A reasonable level of insecurity can be helpful in overcoming dangers, planning more effectively, preparing better for our undertakings, and so on. However, we must all learn to overcome the hindrances of insecurity and move forward in order to excel and to make a difference in our world.

Insecurity makes people overrate their challenges and underestimate their own potential. Highly insecure people are more likely to develop the habit of procrastination and, eventually, become passive.

Man's feeling of insecurity is not new. Many Bible characters felt inadequate about the plan of God for their lives. Gideon was one such person.

Gideon's Struggles

"And the LORD looked upon him, and said, Go in this thy might, and thou shalt save Israel from the hand of the Midianites: have not I sent thee? And he said unto him, Oh my Lord, wherewith shall I save Israel? behold, my family is poor in Manasseh, and I am the least in my father's house" (Judges 6:14–15).

The Bible passage above comes from Gideon's first encounter with God. At the time, the Midianites ruled over the children of Israel and invaded the land in times of harvest. The children of Israel worked hard but remained poor because their oppressor confiscated their harvest and left them with barely enough food to survive.

Naturally, Gideon, like the rest of God's people under oppression at the time, was tired of the oppression and wondered when God would intervene to deliver them from their enemy. He did not know that God was eyeing him to serve as the deliverer of the people.

As the children of Israel prayed and cried to God for help, God decided to appoint a judge to deliver them. He chose Gideon and took steps to reveal His mandate to him.

One day, while Gideon was threshing corn in a winepress to hide his harvest from the Midianites, he had a spiritual encounter with God and heard a clear message to go and deliver the children of Israel from their oppression:

"And the LORD looked upon him, and said, Go in this thy might, and thou shalt save Israel from the hand of the Midianites: have not I sent thee?" (Judges 6:14).

Before we proceed to look closer at Gideon's response, let us quickly pay attention to three significant phrases from the mandate that God gave him.

1. *"...Go in this thy might":* This phrase shows that God saw something in Gideon that was useful for delivering the children of Israel. God called it *"this thy might."* Another way to put it is "this might of yours" or "this ability of yours." The word "might" also means ability, vigor, capacity, or strength. God was referring to something that was already in Gideon: the ability necessary for the accomplishment of the

task. He had this "might," yet he was hiding and living in fear! Do you know what you have?

2. ***"...and thou shalt save Israel":*** In this phrase, God was showing Gideon that the salvation of Israel was in the hands of Gideon. It was up to Gideon to work with God and make it happen. Gideon needed to understand that he had an important role to play in the deliverance of the people. The breakthrough needed was not just up to God. God likes to work with His children to accomplish great things on the earth. He chose Gideon then. He may choose you now!

3. ***"... have not I sent thee?":*** God is saying here that Gideon had His authorization, backing, and support to deliver the people. Gideon was not just about to take on a task according to the will of God. He was going to act on behalf of Heaven. This also meant that he would have the backing and the power of Heaven with him. What does Heaven want you to do with the rest of your life?

The three phrases above show us that God saw Gideon as the right person to take on the task of delivering the children of Israel from their unpleasant situation. He was God's man for the season and the hour. Heaven believed in him, and the timing appeared ripe and right to God.

Yet Gideon did not see the situation as ideal. Like many people today, he had his doubts about his own qualifications and felt insecure and inadequate, as we can read from his reaction below:

Make it Happen!

"And he said unto him, Oh my Lord, wherewith shall I save Israel? behold, my family is poor in Manasseh, and I am the least in my father's house" (Judges 6:15).

What can we see from this response? Let us look closer...

1. ***"... wherewith shall I save Israel?":*** Another way to put Gideon's question is "What will I use to save Israel?" It is a way of saying that he did not see within himself anything that could be useful in saving Israel. This tells us that Gideon did not see his own potential. He did not see the ability that God saw in him, the one that God called "this thy might." Gideon did not know his true potential and did not feel that he was the ideal person to receive such a mandate. He only saw his own limitations, and was particularly concerned about two of them, as we can see from the two phrases below.

2. ***"... my family is poor in Manasseh":*** This phrase shows that Gideon did not see that someone from a poor family like his could save a nation. He had been living with the idea that the ideal deliverer of the people would have to come from a richer family. In his opinion, his family's financial situation disqualified him. He felt that he had the wrong family background for the task. Growing up in poverty made him feel inferior and insecure.

3. ***"... I am the least in my father's house":*** The word "least" in the passage also means

insignificant or less important. He felt that other members of the family had better qualifications for such a mandate.

In Gideon's mind, he did not fit the ideal person, and he did not see anything in his life that would make him capable of saving the people. Insecure people hardly ever see their true potential.

Gideon, like many insecure people, focused on the things that he considered his limitations, making it hard for him to embrace the plan of God for his life and to take the steps necessary for progress.

Prior to his encounter with God, Gideon lived for several years feeling incapable and helpless while struggling and waiting for a time when God would intervene in their situation.

When that time came and God appointed him, he continued to focus on his own limitations instead of making up his mind to act on the authorization from Heaven and to use His potential and the support from God to make things happen. He did not feel that he had the ideal background and circumstances for the task.

Gideon was not conscious of the fact that many of history's great achievers had humble backgrounds. God has the habit of choosing people that appear unqualified in the eyes of the rational world and working with them to touch history.

Make it Happen!

The Bible says...

"For ye see your calling, brethren, how that not many wise men after the flesh, not many mighty, not many noble, are called: But God hath chosen the foolish things of the world to confound the wise; and God hath chosen the weak things of the world to confound the things which are mighty; And base things of the world, and things which are despised, hath God chosen, yea, and things which are not, to bring to nought things that are: That no flesh should glory in his presence" (1 Cor. 1:26-29).

As Gideon struggled with the idea of being God's instrument for delivering the children of Israel from oppression, God reassured him that He would be with Gideon. With God on his side, he had the ideal situation, but he did not realize it.

"And the LORD said unto him, Surely I will be with thee, and thou shalt smite the Midianites as one man" (Judges 6:16).

The message is that Gideon was to deliver the people from the hands of the Midianites with God's support. That was the reassurance that Gideon needed. He had his ideal situation. There is no limit to what you are able to do if you work together with God.

Gideon understood the true meaning of having the ideal situation in life; namely, having God on one's side. How can we see that he understood the power of God's presence? It is easy to see if we read his encounter with the angel more carefully.

Here is a portion to pay attention to:

"And the angel of the LORD appeared unto him, and said unto him, The LORD is with thee, thou mighty man of valour. And Gideon said unto him, Oh my Lord, if the LORD be with us, why then is all this befallen us? and where be all his miracles which our fathers told us of, saying, Did not the LORD bring us up from Egypt? but now the LORD hath forsaken us, and delivered us into the hands of the Midianites" (Judges 6:12-13).

Notice that the angel greeted him by saying, "The Lord is with thee...." Gideon then responded by asking the angel, "Oh my Lord, if the LORD be with us, why then is all this befallen us? And where be all his miracles which our fathers told us of...?" He went on to say, "...the Lord hath forsaken us, and delivered us into the hands of the Midianites." In other words, "Hey, Lord, the Midianites would not be ruling over us right now if God is with us!"

Gideon was right. The Bible tells us that God left His children then because they were living in evil, forcing Him to leave them:

"And the children of Israel did evil in the sight of the LORD: and the LORD delivered them into the hand of Midian seven years. And the hand of Midian prevailed against Israel: and because of the Midianites the children of Israel made them the dens which are in the mountains, and caves, and strong holds" (Judges 6:1-2).

Living in defeat made them hide in dens and caves. The Bible tells us that the Midianites would show up during harvest and take away the yields of the land, leaving the children of Israel in poverty and constant fear.

Such a condition made Gideon thresh wheat in the winepress in the hope of hiding his wheat harvest from the Midianites. The Midianites knew that it was time for the wheat harvest and came to the threshing floors to rob the people. The winepress is the place to go during grape harvest season.

Although the children of Israel lived in a fruitful land with abundance, they suffered poverty!

"And Israel was greatly impoverished because of the Midianites; and the children of Israel cried unto the LORD" (Judges 6:6).

Well, the good news is that the children of Israel eventually became tired of oppression after seven years of fear and poverty. They repented of their sins and turned to God. In His mercy, He decided to deliver them.

However, we know from history that God normally works with human beings to solve problems on the earth. He worked with Noah to begin a cleaner world. He worked with Moses to deliver the children of Israel from bondage in Egypt. He worked with Joshua to take them to the Promised Land.

Wherever there are needs on the earth that God wants to provide for, He will look for a person that is open to receiving His mandate. Once God finds such a person, He will begin to work out His will. Wherever people are hungry, God looks for someone with a compassionate heart to make a difference. He then stirs up the heart of such a person and works with that person to answer the cries of those in need and to alleviate their pain. Is the Lord stirring up your heart to make a difference in an area of need? Are you feeling a special burden or compassion for a person or a people in need? God may be counting on you to work with Him!

In the Lord's determination to set them free, He chose Gideon and gave him a mandate to deliver the children of Israel from their oppression. Gideon felt insecure, but he understood that having God with him would result in absolute victory.

Therefore, he only wanted to be sure of the presence of God in his life. He performed some experiments, took some steps to be sure that God was on his side, and moved into action as he confirmed God's hand on his life. We do not have the time and the space to go into all of the details in this book. Anyone curious about the entire story can start reading the Bible in the book of Judges, chapter six.

Many believers today know the plan of God for their lives but do not take the steps necessary to succeed in God because of insecurity. Such believers focus on the limitations that they sense in their lives and forget about the unlimited power of having God on their side. They feel that they do not fit the profiles of successful people.

As Heaven and the people in need wait for them, they claim to be waiting on Heaven to create the ideal situation or the perfect conditions for them to take

Make it Happen!

steps. In their insecurity, they yearn for more "ideal" situations and live fruitless lives while walking around with great dreams, visions, talents, potential, and heavy burdens in their hearts. You must be different! Surrender your feelings of insecurity to God, yield to His plans, and start moving forward!

3. VICTORY SECRETS OF QUEEN ESTHER

"Then Mordecai commanded to answer Esther, Think not with thyself that thou shalt escape in the king's house, more than all the Jews. For if thou altogether holdest thy peace at this time, then shall there enlargement and deliverance arise to the Jews from another place; but thou and thy father's house shall be destroyed: and who knoweth whether thou art come to the kingdom for such a time as this?" (Est. 4:13–14).

This chapter will show you an event in the life of Queen Esther that will provide you with important keys to help you evaluate difficult situations and possibly identify your place in them. You will also see how she defeated her greatest fear and took the steps necessary to save lives.

Queen Esther grew up with her uncle, Mordecai, before taking part in the beauty contest that landed her in the palace as a queen in a foreign land.

She was a beautiful young Jewish woman in a position of influence, and there was a plot to destroy the Jews. Her uncle thought that her position in the palace might

Make it Happen!

hold the key to saving the lives of the Jews. He wanted her to use her position to approach the king so that he could intervene to stop the evil plot.

A top ranked government official working closely with the king at the time had grown to hate the Jews. With time, the hatred grew stronger and finally reached a level that made him want to see them dead. His name was Haman, and he had a plan in place to destroy the Jews because he saw them as Mordecai's people, a man that he had come to hate deeply.

Haman felt that Mordecai was disrespectful because people normally bowed to greet Haman, but Mordecai refused to bow to him. In Haman's anger against Mordecai, he did not just work out a plan to hang this man; once he found out that Mordecai was a Jew, he decided to destroy all of the Jews in the kingdom!

Here is how the Bible puts it:

"And when Haman saw that Mordecai bowed not, nor did him reverence, then was Haman full of wrath. And he thought scorn to lay hands on Mordecai alone; for they had shewed him the people of Mordecai: wherefore Haman sought to destroy all the Jews that were throughout the whole kingdom of Ahasuerus, even the people of Mordecai" (Est. 3:5-6).

With his mind made up to destroy the Jews, he came up with an accusation against them and spoke to the king about it, and the king left him with authority and discretion to take care of the situation. Haman could not have wished for better!

Here is the Bible passage:

"And Haman said unto king Ahasuerus, There is a certain people scattered abroad and dispersed among the people in all the provinces of thy kingdom; and their laws are diverse from all people; neither keep they the king's laws: therefore it is not for the king's profit to suffer them. If it please the king, let it be written that they may be destroyed: and I will pay ten thousand talents of silver to the hands of those that have the charge of the business, to bring it into the king's treasuries. And the king took his ring from his hand, and gave it unto Haman the son of Hammedatha the Agagite, the Jews' enemy. And the king said unto Haman, The silver is given to thee, the people also, to do with them as it seemeth good to thee" (Est. 3:8–11).

With the backing of the king, Haman called the scribes, wrote in the name of the king, sealed the messages with the king's ring, and sent out dispatchers to all of the provinces in the king's domain with a set date for the total annihilation of the Jews.

"And in every province, whithersoever the king's commandment and his decree came, there was great mourning among the Jews, and fasting, and weeping, and wailing; and many lay in sackcloth and ashes" (Est. 4:3).

The Jews knew that they were in trouble, and they needed God to intervene in the situation. Mordecai was sorrowful and eager to find a solution. He approached the palace, but he had the wrong dress, and protocols did not allow him to get beyond the gate!

Make it Happen!

"When Mordecai perceived all that was done, Mordecai rent his clothes, and put on sackcloth with ashes, and went out into the midst of the city, and cried with a loud and a bitter cry; And came even before the king's gate: for none might enter into the king's gate clothed with sackcloth" (Est. 4:1–2).

Mordecai certainly wanted to let Esther know about the situation.

Although her becoming a queen appeared circumstantial or the result of "good luck" or "good fortune" at the time that she participated and won the beauty contest, her uncle soon began to see that God may have placed her there for reasons beyond her own success and progress.

Esther, the People's Hope

Mordecai felt that his niece, Esther, now the queen of the kingdom, might be the hope of the Jews, and that God planted her in that position to prevent the destruction of the children of Israel.

He sent a copy of the king's message to Queen Esther at the earliest possibility, informing her about the threat against the Jews and requesting her to go to the king to try to prevent the evil.

However, it was not customary for anyone to go to the king without invitation. The penalty of going against the protocol was death, unless the king would stretch out his scepter to save such a person from the security personnel. The queen had to follow the rule just like everyone else.

With no invitation from the king, Queen Esther felt that her uncle's request would endanger her life, and she sent a message back to Mordecai reminding him of the need to have an invitation from the king before going into his presence as well as the possible consequence of attempting to meet the king without such an invitation.

"Again Esther spake unto Hatach, and gave him commandment unto Mordecai; All the king's servants, and the people of the king's provinces, do know, that whosoever, whether man or woman, shall come unto the king into the inner court, who is not called, there is one law of his to put him to death, except such to whom the king shall hold out the golden sceptre, that he may live: but I have not been called to come in unto the king these thirty days" (Est. 4:10-11).

Esther expected her uncle to empathize with her in the situation and understand her challenge, but Mordecai sent another message to her. That is the message in our opening passage. As you can read, her uncle responded with a warning.

"Then Mordecai commanded to answer Esther, Think not with thyself that thou shalt escape in the king's house, more than all the Jews. For if thou altogether holdest thy peace at this time, then shall there enlargement and deliverance arise to the Jews from another place; but thou and thy father's house shall be destroyed: and who knoweth whether thou art come to the kingdom for such a time as this?" (Est. 4:13-14).

Make it Happen!

The Queen loved her people, but she felt that she would be risking her life by going to the king without invitation. She cared about the people, but the fear of possible death stood in her way. She was insecure and had no guarantees about the outcome.

Mordecai saw Esther as the possible solution to the situation, but Esther saw fear and possible personal destruction. The uncle's request was like calling on her to commit suicide. She respected him, but dying was not on her agenda at that time.

A naturally ideal situation then would have been for the king to invite her. A better ideal situation would have been for someone else to take care of that problem without involving her. The best ideal situation would have been for the problem not to exist in the first place!

She had no suicide in mind when she signed up for the beauty contest that landed her in the palace. She did not enroll to be an activist. Being a martyr was never her ambition, and she had no admiration for death.

Judging from the love of Mordecai for Esther, we can conclude that the uncle also had no intention to see her die. However, the situation was desperate, and he saw Esther having the potential to save the Jews because of her position as a queen. He was not seeking her death. He was simply desperately looking for ways to save the Jews.

Some people run around in search of their destinies. Others come face to face with their destinies under unforeseen circumstances, wrapped in unattractive packages! Esther was having a blind date with a part of her destiny, and she did not like the look of it! Winning a great beauty contest was pleasant, but she did not foresee that it was going to bring her into such a difficult situation. Promotions come with additional responsibilities, and progress brings new challenges.

Most Bible students know that Esther finally overcame her fears and took the necessary steps. The question is, "How?" What was the secret of her victory? How does a person in such a difficult situation defeat personal insecurities, understand the will of God, and work in partnership with God to make things happen?

To understand the secret of Queen Esther's victory in this tough situation, we must pay attention to her communication with her beloved uncle, Mordecai.

Lessons from Mordecai's Message to Esther

For convenience, let us read Mordecai's reply to Esther's initial refusal one more time:

"Then Mordecai commanded to answer Esther, Think not with thyself that thou shalt escape in the king's house, more than all the Jews. For if thou altogether holdest thy peace at this time, then shall there enlargement and deliverance arise to the Jews from another place; but thou and thy father's house shall be destroyed: and who knoweth whether thou art come to the kingdom for such a time as this?" (Est. 4:13–14).

In the above passage, we can see that Mordecai successfully made two principles clear to Esther, resulting in her breakthrough. Understand these principles, and you will begin to see challenges in new ways. Here they are in today's simple language:

1. ***God may have a purpose for promoting you:*** Mordecai tried to make her understand that God must have been behind her promotion for a purpose. Promotions from God usually follow times of a faithful walk with Him and normally result in greater responsibilities and challenges.

If you are faithful, God will promote you. If He promotes you, then your responsibilities, challenges, and privileges will increase! If you are faithful in the new responsibilities, challenges, and privileges, you will experience more victories and promotions, leading to more responsibilities, challenges, and privileges!

Moving higher will bring you in contact with people of higher levels, but it will also make those in need look in your direction for help. The crown attracts the crowd. Wealth attracts people with needs. Successful people hardly enjoy successes just by themselves. Many of them carry the burdens of other people and have sleepless nights because of the pains of less privileged acquaintances and strangers.

Mordecai's viewpoint has support in many other Bible passages. Here are some of them:

"For promotion cometh neither from the east, nor from the west, nor from the south. But God is the judge: he putteth down one, and setteth up another" (Ps. 75:6–7).

"He raiseth up the poor out of the dust, and lifteth the needy out of the dunghill; That he may set him with princes, even with the princes of his people. He maketh the barren woman to keep house, and to be a joyful mother of children. Praise ye the LORD" (Ps. 113:7–9).

"Yet setteth he the poor on high from affliction, and maketh him families like a flock" (Ps. 107:41).

"I would seek unto God, and unto God would I commit my cause: Which doeth great things and unsearchable; marvellous things without number: Who giveth rain upon the earth, and sendeth waters upon the fields: To set up on high those that be low; that those which mourn may be exalted to safety" (Job 5:8–11).

Learn to always remember that God has more than your personal happiness in mind when He promotes you. He is counting on you to touch lives beyond you. Live up to His purpose and expectations faithfully and consistently, and you will continue to have promotions.

2. ***See what is truly at stake:*** Esther worried about her own safety, and she had good reasons for it, but she forgot to see the fact that all of the Jews were in danger and that they were depending on her for their safety. She needed to see beyond herself and look at the needs of the people under her care.

Make it Happen!

With the lives of an entire people at stake, Queen Esther could not afford to simply turn down her uncle's request. She needed to see the bigger picture and realize that the stakes were too high for playing it "safe" selfishly.

God always has the option of finding someone else to do something when the person with the first opportunity to do it fails, and Mordecai was quick to let Esther know that help may come to the Jews in another way if she refused to do her part. That would be failure on her part, and she would be out of line with the purpose of God for her life, risking her own downfall and possible death!

Great achievers understand the importance of seeing the bigger picture and seeing what is truly at stake.

Moses saw what was truly at stake when he led the children of Israel in the wilderness and heard about God's intention to destroy them. At the time, God was angry with them because of their stubbornness. While Moses was up on the mountain receiving instructions from God for Israel, the people concluded that Moses was already dead, and they decided to make a god in the form of a golden calf to take them back to Egypt. To them, Moses was away for too long to still be alive.

God was angry with them for their idolatry and told Moses about His intention to destroy them:

"And the LORD said unto Moses, I have seen this people, and, behold, it is a stiffnecked people: Now therefore let me alone, that my wrath may wax hot against them, and

that I may consume them: and I will make of thee a great nation" (Ex. 32:9-10).

Notice in the passage above that Moses was not even in danger. God was going to destroy the people and make a new beginning with Moses. God was offering Moses an opportunity to be free from a troublesome people, but as we are about to see from the reaction of Moses, this man was not selfish at all. He looked beyond his own interest, saw the bigger picture, and noticed what was truly at stake.

Here is how Moses responded to the message from God:

"And Moses besought the LORD his God, and said, LORD, why doth thy wrath wax hot against thy people, which thou hast brought forth out of the land of Egypt with great power, and with a mighty hand? Wherefore should the Egyptians speak, and say, For mischief did he bring them out, to slay them in the mountains, and to consume them from the face of the earth? Turn from thy fierce wrath, and repent of this evil against thy people. Remember Abraham, Isaac, and Israel, thy servants, to whom thou swarest by thine own self, and saidst unto them, I will multiply your seed as the stars of heaven, and all this land that I have spoken of will I give unto your seed, and they shall inherit it for ever. And the LORD repented of the evil which he thought to do unto his people" (Ex. 32:11-14).

From the response above, we can see that Moses cared about the people and that he cared about the reputation of God. He did not want any situation that would give reasons to other people to speak evil of the

Lord. He felt that the Egyptians would have a reason to mock the Lord. Moses understood that the lives of the children of Israel and the reputation of the Lord were at stake.

Paul the Apostle was willing to trade his own salvation for the salvation of his people:

"I say the truth in Christ, I lie not, my conscience also bearing me witness in the Holy Ghost, That I have great heaviness and continual sorrow in my heart. For I could wish that myself were accursed from Christ for my brethren, my kinsmen according to the flesh" (Rom. 9:1-3).

Great achievers succeed in life because they think beyond their own personal needs. They try to take steps to meet the needs of their family members, their communities, their nations, and their world. They think about the future and seize the moment with the bigger picture in mind.

Most of the inventors in the pages of history books made great advances because they wanted to make life better for all of us. They wanted us to enjoy electricity, travel faster and safer, communicate across continents, live healthier, and simply enjoy life. They saw that the status quo would keep people in darkness, make them spend too much time to reach their destinations, cause people to suffer illnesses, and waste precious lives. They saw the future of humanity's efficiencies and effectiveness at stake and could not just live their lives without trying to make a difference.

Moved by needs beyond their own, they made personal sacrifices, investing time, money, and energy to conduct researches for the good of their world. The great technologies that we enjoy today are the results of the commitment of a relatively few people who were willing to look beyond their own needs and see what was truly at stake.

To make greater things happen, you must see needs beyond your own. You need to see and feel the pain, struggles, and predicaments of other people. These people may be your family members, friends, colleagues, tribesmen, industry, community, state, nation, and so on. Learn to think about the possible positive impact that your success will likely have on their lives, and you will feel a strong sense of responsibility and motivation to take difficult steps.

> **3. *Taking a calculated risk may be the safest thing to do:*** Mordecai reminded the queen that she was also a Jew and that she was already in danger. Esther felt too secure in her palace to understand that killing the Jews also meant that she would die too.

We must not make light of her plight. The fact is that going to the king without his invitation was quite risky. She had no assurance that the king would stretch out the scepter to save her life if she would approach him without his invitation.

However, Mordecai made her understand that playing it "safe" by refusing to go to the king was naïve. He said that it would certainly result in her death! He made her understand that she was in a situation that necessitated her taking a calculated risk.

Refusing to take the risks for going to the king without his invitation was equal to accepting the predicament of sure death. The risk of going to the king had some possibilities of success. Whenever we have to choose between guaranteed failure for taking no risks and some chances of success for taking risks, we must lean towards the risks with chances of success.

Doing nothing is not always safer than doing something. One must weigh the options realistically. No one can walk with God without the willingness to take "risks." Taking a risk approved by God may be the safest thing to do in a difficult situation. The ability to evaluate and calculate risks properly and wisely, and the courage and faith to choose the right kind of risk are essential for our safety and progress.

Calculating risks properly can help us to replace fear with faith and move us forward in difficult situations.

Mordecai's message found a place in Queen Esther's heart and mind, and she finally went beyond her fears! She decided to take the risks!

The "If I Perish, I Perish" Mentality

Esther's breakthrough came when she made the decision to confront her own fears and take the right kind of risk. She overcame her own self and took on what we call the "if I perish, I perish" mentality! We shall see this mentality in a moment, but first, let us read the next part of her message to Mordecai.

"Then Esther bade them return Mordecai this answer, Go, gather together all the Jews that are present in Shushan, and fast ye for me, and neither eat nor drink three days, night or day: I also and my maidens will fast likewise; and so will I go in unto the king, which is not according to the law: and if I perish, I perish" (Est. 4:15-16).

The queen made the difficult decision to go to the king and report the matter. Hold on a minute! Take a moment to meditate on the fact that she was not just impulsive with her decision. She calculated the risk and realized that doing nothing would mean perishing and that doing something might lead to safety. This is wisdom. Remember that God does not bless foolishness!

After calculating her risks, she asked for spiritual cover by requesting that the Jews pray and fast along with her for three days. She understood that most of the things that happen in the world have a spiritual dimension to them. She understood the importance of having God's support and took steps to gain spiritual advantage in the situation. Prayer connects us to God and strengthens us in our weaknesses.

Queen Esther's "if I perish, I perish" mentality opened the door for her to experience the favor of God and to see the hand of God in action. Many people do not get the chance to see God's abilities in their lives and in their circumstances because they do not take the steps necessary for Him to show up!

Queen Esther confronted her own fears and took the step after a time of prayer and fasting:

"Now it came to pass on the third day, that Esther put on her royal apparel, and stood in the inner court of the king's house, over against the king's house: and the king sat upon his royal throne in the royal house, over against the gate of the house. And it was so, when the king saw Esther the queen standing in the court, that she obtained favour in his sight: and the king held out to Esther the golden sceptre that was in his hand. So Esther drew near, and touched the top of the sceptre. Then said the king unto her, What wilt thou, queen Esther? and what is thy request? it shall be even given thee to the half of the kingdom" (Est. 5:1–3).

This experience was the beginning of breakthroughs for the Jews. Eventually, none of the Jews died. God used Esther to turn the situation around in favor of the Jews.

Now, let us look at what I call the "if I perish, I perish" mentality more closely. It is simple. This mentality describes the attitude of a person that is no longer yielding to the force of fear. It usually follows a careful consideration of the options available in a difficult situation. Such a person then mentally makes a tough decision, consciously aware that such a decision may result in the payment of a high price.

Esther got to this point, and she had the willingness to pay the highest possible price necessary to reach her goals. With her life and that of an entire people at stake, the ultimate price was death. She was aware of this and was willing to die if necessary!

To understand this mentality more effectively, let us look at the breakthrough involving four lepers in the Old Testament:

A long time ago, in the days of Prophet Elisha, the army of Syria surrounded Israel. The Syrians camped strategically and watched the land to restrict the movement of the children of Israel. The siege continued until there was a severe famine in the land.

There were four lepers near the gate of Samaria. They were also out of food supplies and were about to make a very risky but essential decision. We must remember that lepers usually lived outside of the cities in those days in order to prevent the spread of leprosy in the land. Entering the city as a leper carried the death penalty back then. In their case, there were even bigger risks involved in entering the city, namely, famine.

They had three options. They could remain in their present situation and die for sure. They could enter the city and face the possibility of dying because of the famine in the city. The third option was to go to the camp of the Syrians. They were sure that the Syrians had food, but they also knew that the Syrians could kill them!

Let us read their deliberations and see how the "if I perish, I perish" mentality helped them in their decision:

Make it Happen!

"And there were four leprous men at the entering in of the gate: and they said one to another, Why sit we here until we die? If we say, We will enter into the city, then the famine is in the city, and we shall die there: and if we sit still here, we die also. Now therefore come, and let us fall unto the host of the Syrians: if they save us alive, we shall live; and if they kill us, we shall but die" (2 Kings 7:3–4).

After considering their options, they realized that going to the Syrians could save their lives, but they also knew that the Syrians could kill them. The other two options—accepting the status quo and staying where they were or going into the city in severe famine—would result in sure death. Going to the Syrians had the risk of death, but there was also the possibility of food supply and escape from the famine.

They decided *"…Now therefore, come and let us fall into the host of the Syrians: if they save us alive, we shall live; and if they kill us, we shall but die."* This is the "if I perish, I perish" mentality in action.

Faced with sure death for doing nothing, they decided to take a chance in the direction of a possible breakthrough. They were ready to die on their own terms. However, God went ahead of them, and they did not die!

"And they rose up in the twilight, to go unto the camp of the Syrians: and when they were come to the uttermost part of the camp of Syria, behold, there was no man there. For the Lord had made the host of the Syrians to hear a noise of chariots, and a noise of horses, even the noise of a great host: and they said one to another, Lo,

the king of Israel hath hired against us the kings of the Hittites, and the kings of the Egyptians, to come upon us. Wherefore they arose and fled in the twilight, and left their tents, and their horses, and their asses, even the camp as it was, and fled for their life. And when these lepers came to the uttermost part of the camp, they went into one tent, and did eat and drink, and carried thence silver, and gold, and raiment, and went and hid it; and came again, and entered into another tent, and carried thence also, and went and hid it" (2 Kings 7:5–8).

These lepers did not only find great wealth but they ended up saving lives in the city! Those that take chances often make a difference in lives beyond their own!

"Then they said one to another, We do not well: this day is a day of good tidings, and we hold our peace: if we tarry till the morning light, some mischief will come upon us: now therefore come, that we may go and tell the king's household. So they came and called unto the porter of the city: and they told them, saying, We came to the camp of the Syrians, and, behold, there was no man there, neither voice of man, but horses tied, and asses tied, and the tents as they were" (2 Kings 7:9–10).

The "if I perish, I perish" mentality helped the lepers to make the tough decision of moving forward in the midst of danger. They knew that death was also part of the other alternatives. Therefore, the wise thing to do was to calculate the costs and choose wisely and courageously.

We can see another example in the lives of Shadrach, Meshach, and Abednego. They were Hebrews in exile

Make it Happen!

in the days of King Nebuchadnezzar. The king set a gold image for the inhabitants of the kingdom to worship, but these Hebrews, believing in God, refused to serve images and other gods. The king threatened them with death in the burning furnace and gave them the chance that he would allow them to live if they bowed, but they refused to obey the king.

What was the secret of their courage? They had the "if I perish, I perish" mentality!

"Shadrach, Meshach, and Abednego, answered and said to the king, O Nebuchadnezzar, we are not careful to answer thee in this matter. If it be so, our God whom we serve is able to deliver us from the burning fiery furnace, and he will deliver us out of thine hand, O king. But if not, be it known unto thee, O king, that we will not serve thy gods, nor worship the golden image which thou hast set up" (Dan. 3:16–18).

They felt that God was able to deliver them, and they trusted Him to deliver them, but they were willing to die if necessary.

The "if I perish, I perish" mentality helped them to remain true to their faith and to stand their ground in the will of God and in the face of an imminent danger. God stood with them and protected them, and King Nebuchadnezzar promoted them after seeing the power of God!

"Then Nebuchadnezzar spake, and said, Blessed be the God of Shadrach, Meshach, and Abednego, who hath sent his angel, and delivered his servants that trusted in him, and have changed the king's word, and yielded their

bodies, that they might not serve nor worship any god, except their own God. Therefore I make a decree, That every people, nation, and language, which speak any thing amiss against the God of Shadrach, Meshach, and Abednego, shall be cut in pieces, and their houses shall be made a dunghill: because there is no other God that can deliver after this sort. Then the king promoted Shadrach, Meshach, and Abednego, in the province of Babylon" (Dan. 3:28–30).

The Lord Jesus Christ is the ultimate example of this mentality. The Bible teaches us that He came into this world to die for our sins. After living for about thirty years and spending around three years with His disciples, He felt the time of His death drawing nearer. Although dying was on His agenda when He came into the world, the decision to proceed in the face of death was tough. He felt sorrow and pain, and he felt the temptation to abandon the mission, but He pressed forward.

Let us see His experience and observe how He made the difficult choice:

"Then saith he unto them, My soul is exceeding sorrowful, even unto death: tarry ye here, and watch with me. And he went a little further, and fell on his face, and prayed, saying, O my Father, if it be possible, let this cup pass from me: nevertheless not as I will, but as thou wilt. And he cometh unto the disciples, and findeth them asleep, and saith unto Peter, What, could ye not watch with me one hour? Watch and pray, that ye enter not into temptation: the spirit indeed is willing, but the flesh is weak. He went away again the second time, and prayed, saying, O my Father, if this cup may not pass

away from me, except I drink it, thy will be done" (Matt. 26:38-42).

His human feelings were working against His destiny, but He prevailed by submitting His feelings to the will of His Heavenly Father. He was willing to pay the ultimate price. He died, rose again on the third day, and opened the door of salvation to the entire world. Prayer helped Him through His darkest moments and strengthened His ability to decide with the "if I perish, I perish" mentality. That is why He was able to say, *"O my Father, if this cup may not pass away from me, except I drink it, thy will be done."*

The Bible encourages us to follow the Lord's example with the right mentality and the determination to obey God at all costs:

"Let this mind be in you, which was also in Christ Jesus: Who, being in the form of God, thought it not robbery to be equal with God: But made himself of no reputation, and took upon him the form of a servant, and was made in the likeness of men: And being found in fashion as a man, he humbled himself, and became obedient unto death, even the death of the cross" (Phil. 2:5-8).

Paul the Apostle also had the same "if I perish, I perish" mentality. While on His way to Jerusalem, the Holy Spirit indicated that he would face bondage and afflictions there, but He did not allow the fear of paying a high price to stop him from obeying the pull that he was sensing deep within him as he felt "bound in the spirit" to go to Jerusalem:

"And now, behold, I go bound in the spirit unto Jerusalem, not knowing the things that shall befall me there: Save that the Holy Ghost witnesseth in every city, saying that bonds and afflictions abide me. But none of these things move me, neither count I my life dear unto myself, so that I might finish my course with joy, and the ministry, which I have received of the Lord Jesus, to testify the gospel of the grace of God" (Acts 20:22-24).

He was unwavering in his determination to move forward because he had the "if I perish, I perish" mentality. He was willing to risk his life in order to fulfill the ministry and accomplish the plan of God for his life. As a result, he became one of the most fruitful apostles of all time.

The "if I perish, I perish" mentality does not always have to involve death. It may involve a continued life of poverty, living outside of one's true passion and dreams, and living far away from the purpose of God.

The "if I perish, I perish" mentality simply means being ready to pay the highest price necessary for the possibility of a breakthrough in a tough situation. To make things happen, you must be willing to pay the price necessary for your progress.

Most of the difficult situations keeping people away from progress do not involve death. Their risks are far lower than the risks of Queen Esther; the four lepers; Shadrach, Meshach, and Abednego; the Lord Jesus Christ; and Paul the Apostle. The prices that most people have to pay to make things happen are far lower. To some people, the price is the additional workload of starting a course while already having a busy work schedule. To others, it may mean relocating to another country.

To some people, the price may mean giving up one or more television programs, sacrificing their vacation plans, and sleeping less! One person's price may sound like a luxury to another person, but everyone with the desire to make great things happen must be willing to pay the price! What price are you willing to pay in order to accomplish the next level in the progress plan of God for your life?

Combine Wisdom, Spirituality, and Faith

Wisdom, spirituality, and faith must work together in our efforts to walk in the "if I perish, I perish" mentality. Some people work with "wisdom" and do not reach their goals because they undermine spirituality and faith. Others are super spiritual, but they lack wisdom.

There are also many people with "faith" that act impulsively without using wisdom and making the necessary spiritual preparations for their actions. Queen Esther combined all three, which needs to be done if you want to excel in the will of God for your life.

> 1. **Wisdom:** Wisdom is the proper and effective use of knowledge. Wisdom helped Queen Esther and the lepers to analyze their options and make the right choices.

Speaking of wisdom, the Bible says:

"Wisdom is the principal thing; therefore get wisdom: and with all thy getting get understanding" (Prov. 4:7).

"How much better is it to get wisdom than gold! and to get understanding rather to be chosen than silver!" (Prov. 16:16).

"If any of you lack wisdom, let him ask of God, that giveth to all men liberally, and upbraideth not; and it shall be given him" (James 1:5).

2. **Spirituality:** Spirituality is conforming to spiritual laws and walking in spiritual principles. This is why Queen Esther took some time to pray and fast. This is the reason why the Lord Jesus took time to pray in one of His darkest moments.

The Bible says:

"Pray without ceasing" (1 Thess. 5:17).

"Be careful for nothing; but in every thing by prayer and supplication with thanksgiving let your requests be made known unto God" (Phil. 4:6).

3. **Faith:** Faith allows us to do the right thing, trusting God for the best outcome, in His will. Faith moves us into actions even when we do not have any sure evidence of our wishes or desires. Faith moved Queen Esther to go to the king without his invitation, hoping and believing that he would stretch out his scepter

to save her life. Faith moved the four lepers into the camp of the Syrians, hoping and believing that the foreigners would spare their lives and give them food to eat.

Many people do not take major steps to achieve greater goals in life because they allow fears to cripple them. They see and sometimes imagine extreme dangers out there, even when situations are not quite as grim as they imagine! Consequently, they remain slothful or inactive, procrastinating consistently and living far below their potential.

The Bible puts it clearly:

"The slothful man saith, There is a lion without, I shall be slain in the streets" (Prov. 22:13).

Such people prefer to keep the status quo, stay in a constant state of indecision, and never take on new adventures. They are creative at imagining extreme dangers and are never able to defeat their fears.

When it comes to progress, everyone willing to achieve great things with God must learn to be adventurous. When you walk with God, you may go through the *storm* or through *fire*, but He promises to protect you.

"But now thus saith the LORD that created thee, O Jacob, and he that formed thee, O Israel, Fear not: for I have redeemed thee, I have called thee by thy name; thou art mine. When thou passest through the waters, I will be with thee; and through the rivers, they shall not overflow thee: when thou walkest through the fire, thou shalt not

be burned; neither shall the flame kindle upon thee" (Is. 43:1-2).

We must combine wisdom, spirituality, and faith in order to make things happen in this world. Take the steps necessary in your current challenge, and you will pave the way for the breakthrough that God has in place for you. One breakthrough will pave the way for the next breakthrough as you remain faithful, and your life will continue to prosper on the path of progress.

4. HOW TO QUALIFY FOR YOUR NEXT LEVEL

"But in a great house there are not only vessels of gold and of silver, but also of wood and of earth; and some to honour, and some to dishonour. If a man therefore purge himself from these, he shall be a vessel unto honour, sanctified, and meet for the master's use, and prepared unto every good work" (2 Tim. 2:20–21).

The first chapter of this book shows that we do not need to wait for everything around us to be "perfect" before we take steps. We can overcome procrastination and work God's great goals in the midst of challenges as long as we have Him on our side. The second chapter shows that we can use vital lessons from the life of Gideon to overcome personal insecurities and fulfill the plan of God. We then went on in chapter three to learn precious lessons about taking difficult steps by looking into a difficult moment in the life of Queen Esther.

The next thing that we need to understand before moving forward in this book is the concept of qualification. The understanding of this concept is essential in our time because of the misconceptions among God's people about the subject of grace. Many believers feel that the grace of God is there to take care of their success and think that they do not need to do much on their part. They ignore important principles of progress in the Scriptures and do not realize that most of the promises in the Bible have conditions for God's people to fulfill before such promises materialize.

Our opening passage says that a great house may have vessels of gold, silver, wood, and earth (clay) and that some of these vessels are for honor while others are for dishonor. The great house here is God's house, and the vessels are the people. This means that some people are useful to serve honorably, while others do not have the same usefulness.

Being honorable is a matter of choice.

The first impression after reading the opening passage is to think that the master of the house randomly chose and assigned honorable and dishonorable functions to each of these vessels without any efforts of their own. However, if we pay close attention to the last part of the passage, it will become clear that the believer has a role to play.

"If a man therefore purge himself from these, he shall be a vessel unto honour, sanctified, and meet for the master's use, and prepared unto every good work" (2 Tim. 2:21).

Pay close attention and notice the conditional "If..." in the sentence. It shows that a man can purge himself and become a vessel of honor, sanctified and ready for the master's use. In other words, God is not the only one determining the outcome of a person's life.

God created each individual with different kinds of qualities and potential in just the same sense as gold, silver, wood, and clay are unique and different in their characteristics, but each individual can be honorable by choice.

Every person can choose to be a *"vessel unto honor"* by going through purging, sanctification, and preparation for the Master's use.

We must pay attention to the following four portions of the verse in order to understand the secret principle of the verse:

1. **Purging:** *"If a man therefore purge himself from these...."* The word purge here means to clean up or clean out. It means to get rid of the wrong things. Look closely and you will notice *"from these."*

The next logical question, then, is, "What does the word "these" in the passage refer to?" To answer that question, we must look at earlier verses, notably, from verse 16 to verse 19 of 2 Timothy, chapter 2, and the verses after verse 21 of the same chapter.

Based on the content of the other verses, we can conclude that *"these"* refers to profane and vain babblings, ungodliness, false teachings, shipwreck of faith, iniquity, youthful lusts, foolish and unlearned questions, strife, and the snares of the devil. Habitually entertaining such things hinders people from progressing in God and makes it impossible for them to live, serve, and progress honorably.

Therefore, anyone who wants to be honorable must be free of such things. We must apply the truth of the word of God in our lives and develop healthy habits based on the principles contained in the word of God.

2. **Sanctification:** To sanctify means to make holy or to set aside. Sanctification is a spiritual experience that cleanses a person and sets such a person aside for a distinct life of service in the will of God.

This experience redefines how a person values, prioritizes, and focuses on the things of this life, making such a person serve God more naturally. This empowerment makes it normal for people to think and act in line with the standard of God.

Sanctification usually follows a life of personal dedication and commitment to the purpose of God.

3. **Meet for the Master's use:** The word "meet" also means fit, appropriate, or suitable. The word "use" in the passage means usefulness in the sense of being profitable, needed, or essential. To be *"meet for the Master's use"* means to be fit or suitable for profitable usefulness in line with the intentions of the Master.

From the above, we can see that the progress of every person depends not just on God, but also on the

Make it Happen!

specific efforts of such a person. God wants to use His children honorably, but He can only take them as high as they are willing to go with Him.

> **4. Preparation:** The last part of the verse says, *"and prepared unto every good work."* The word "prepared" in the verse means to make ready and immediately available. It implies being ready before opportunities come our way.

As you can imagine, those that wait for professional and lucrative job vacancies before going to school to learn the trades necessary to qualify them for such vacancies will not have the qualifications necessary to apply for the jobs. To make use of future vacancies, one must prepare ahead. A person's ability to use today's opportunities often depends on the kind of preparations that such a person has made in anticipation of today.

The word "good" in the verse means beneficial. It refers to the kind of work that meets needs, makes differences in people, transforms lives, adds value to societies, and so on. The word "work" in the verse refers to undertaking, doing, deed, activity, or labor.

Put simply, a person that goes through purging by staying away from the things that hinder people from progress will experience sanctification. In addition, through special experiences with God and by becoming different from others in mentality, focus, values, and so on, that person will become useful to the Master after effective preparation, ready to use opportunities for beneficial undertakings. Such a person will live honorably as "gold," "silver," "wood," or "clay" in the house of God and in the plan of God.

Your progress does not only depend on God!

One of the biggest mistakes that believers are making today on the subject of progress is that they assume God to be fully and solely responsible for their progress. They believe that whatever God intends to do will happen.

They think that they only need to pray and let God take care of their progress. Some believe that they only need to put some money in the offering boxes of their churches or give money to some spiritual leaders, and then they can expect guaranteed success. They forget that they also have parts to play in the plan of God for their lives.

Because they believe that progress is all up to God, they also feel that things fail only because God wants them to fail. Therefore, whenever things do not work out, they simply conclude that it was not the will of God.

They forget that they must also recognize their roles in the plan of God and do their parts fully in order to fulfill His purpose and make things happen for the glory of His name and the positive improvement and transformation of lives. They seek divine promotions without yielding to divine preparations. They look for opportunities without preparing to show their qualifications.

They watch others in the world planning smartly and working hard, and they feel that the children of God do not need to work on the land, research the markets, learn progress principles, understand negotiations, and review efforts. They assume that they only need to focus on spiritual matters.

Consequently, they experience stagnation, live below their potential, and watch opportunities walk away from them because they lack the qualifications necessary to utilize such opportunities. Meanwhile, they stay on the same level for a long time as they watch their worldly friends advancing in life.

They then begin to question and doubt the faithfulness of God, complaining that God is not answering their prayers, and feeling that life is not fair!

They want God to grant them exceptions to the rules of progress and to exempt them from the requirements necessary for every opportunity. They spend most of their days listening to Gospel music, watching Christian television, and talking about the Gospel singers leading the latest charts and the preachers pulling in the crowds, but they fail to learn how to identify their own unique qualities and to work out clear and practical steps for their own progress.

They forget that there is a time and place for everything, including Gospel music and Christian television! They fail to realize that God honors qualifications. There is nothing wrong with listening to anointed Gospel music and watching life-enriching Christian television, but these cannot replace the need for us to do our part in our walk with God.

There is a time to pray, a time to plan, and a time to work towards those plans. We must go beyond saying "Amen!" to the promises of God and actually take specific actions towards their fulfillment.

Understand the Concept of Qualification in the Kingdom of God

Qualification has to do with meeting conditions or requirements in order to receive a privilege, occupy a position, receive a title, or perform a function. In a simple sense, to qualify means to meet requirements. A qualified person is one that meets the requirements for something. An unqualified person is someone that does not meet the requirements.

Every mission requires certain qualities and conditions to succeed. Every task requires certain qualifications to perform. Place someone without the right qualifications in a great position within an organization, and the goals of the organization will suffer the consequences of having such an unsuitable person in the position. On the other hand, place the right person in the position, and the organization will have a better chance of reaching its goals. The need to have qualified people in place is one of the main reasons why Human Resource managers scrutinize job applicants critically.

Make it Happen!

Nations, businesses, and church organizations rise and fall by their attitudes towards the concept of qualification. Many countries operate below their potential and fail to excel because they have unqualified people in strategic positions. It is common in such countries to see government officials place unqualified workers in important positions as a means of showing personal favor to such workers.

Most people, including believers, would agree that such decisions are not in the best interests of public institutions, but many believers seem to expect God to do the same thing. They feel that they simply need to have the favor of God on their lives in order to progress in life. They want God to set aside His principles, adjust His expectations, eliminate the need for the natural laws, and so on, just to show that He is their Heavenly Father.

The favor of God is great because it opens doors and gives us extraordinary opportunities, but it does not take away the need for us to qualify.

Many Christians today are unaware of the fact that God respects, teaches, and demands qualifications. They assume that the death and resurrection of the Lord Jesus Christ automatically qualifies them to receive all of the blessings of God, by His grace, without the need for them to do anything on their part. Therefore, they simply pray, remain active in church, and wait for God to help them reach their goals. They forget that faith without works is dead!

These believers ignore opportunities to qualify for promotions; they hide from the responsibilities that they must carry out for their own progress and the progress of the Kingdom of God, and then secretly cry in their hearts and wonder why God is taking "so long" to answer their prayers or to help them.

They expect promotions without qualifications and favor without character. They want harvest without tilling the land, and they seek blessings without making clear commitments to walk on the path of obedience. They desire purity without consecrating their lives, and they look forward to having an abundance of money without reasonable investments. This is because they lack true understanding of the subject of qualification.

Let it be clear: God does not promote people without the right qualifications. Do not just take my word for it; let us examine the Bible more closely, and you will be able to make your own conclusion. You will see that even salvation requires qualification! Yes, you read it correctly. I know that it sounds strange, but before you accuse me of spreading wrong teachings, read on with an open mind, and examine the Bible passages applicable to the subject.

Do not get me wrong. Salvation is the gift of God. However, no one can receive this gift without the right qualifications. There are conditions in place for receiving the gift of salvation. Anyone attempting to receive the gift without meeting these qualifications will fail! Therefore, the gift is only available to those that meet the qualifications that God has in place. Everyone can qualify, but each person must make use of the ability to qualify and actually act to meet the

Make it Happen!

requirements in place by God before they can receive the gift of salvation!

What are the qualifications? The Bible shows us two main qualifications:

(1) Repent of sins
(2) Believe on the Lord Jesus Christ

No sinner can receive the gift of salvation without meeting these conditions. Read the Bible passages below carefully, and notice the conditions or qualifications in them:

"And saying, The time is fulfilled, and the kingdom of God is at hand: repent ye, and believe the gospel" (Mark 1:15).

"Testifying both to the Jews, and also to the Greeks, repentance toward God, and faith toward our Lord Jesus Christ" (Acts 20:21).

"I tell you, Nay: but, except ye repent, ye shall all likewise perish" (Luke 13:5).

"Repent ye therefore, and be converted, that your sins may be blotted out, when the times of refreshing shall come from the presence of the Lord" (Acts 3:19).

"And they said, Believe on the Lord Jesus Christ, and thou shalt be saved, and thy house"
(Acts 16:31).

"Therefore being justified by faith, we have peace with God through our Lord Jesus Christ: By whom also we

have access by faith into this grace wherein we stand, and rejoice in hope of the glory of God" (Rom. 5:1-2).

"Jesus saith unto him, I am the way, the truth, and the life: no man cometh unto the Father, but by me" (John 14:6).

As you may have noticed from the passages above, no one can claim salvation without meeting God's qualifications. No hard work, sacrifices, or efforts made outside of the required conditions can earn anyone salvation. Therefore, the person that wants to receive salvation must pay special attention to the conditions necessary for receiving salvation.

Those who want to excel in health must study the conditions necessary for healthy living. Those who want to achieve great heights in the sciences, ministry, business, career, and other areas need to pay attention to and develop the qualities necessary for progress in the areas of their interests.

The people who understand this principle of qualification and doing their part to qualify for the opportunities that they desire in life are more likely to prosper and reach their goals, whether they are believers or simply ambitious unbelievers.

Make it Happen!

Most Great Promises in the Bible come with Conditions

A careful student of the Bible will see that most of the great promises in the word of God have conditions in place for their fulfillment.

Those receiving the promises and intending to see their fulfillment must meet the conditions in order to receive their benefits. It takes more than just shouting "Amen! Hallelujah! I receive it! I claim it, in the name of Jesus!" for it to happen. We must pay close attention to the conditions and do our part to fulfill those conditions.

Let us quickly read some great promises in the Bible and see if we can identify the conditions necessary for their fulfillment:

"And all these blessings shall come on thee, and overtake thee, if thou shalt hearken unto the voice of the LORD thy God. Blessed shalt thou be in the city, and blessed shalt thou be in the field. Blessed shall be the fruit of thy body, and the fruit of thy ground, and the fruit of thy cattle, the increase of thy kine, and the flocks of thy sheep. Blessed shall be thy basket and thy store. Blessed shalt thou be when thou comest in, and blessed shalt thou be when thou goest out. The LORD shall cause thine enemies that rise up against thee to be smitten before thy face: they shall come out against thee one way, and flee before thee seven ways. The LORD shall command the blessing upon thee in thy storehouses, and in all that thou settest thine hand unto; and he shall bless thee in the land which the LORD thy God giveth thee. The LORD

shall establish thee an holy people unto himself, as he hath sworn unto thee, if thou shalt keep the commandments of the LORD thy God, and walk in his ways. And all people of the earth shall see that thou art called by the name of the LORD; and they shall be afraid of thee" (Deut. 28:2-10).

This passage contains precious promises of great blessings from God to His children.

However, notice the condition: *"...if thou shalt hearken unto the voice of the LORD thy God"* (Deut. 8:2).

The passage is saying that to receive the blessings, the children of Israel must adhere to the voice of the Lord. This means that they had to hear and obey His word. The great blessings were not going to come on them automatically. They had to qualify through knowledge and obedience. It was up to them individually to make the blessings happen in their own lives.

Without hearing and doing His word, they would have no lawful claim on the blessings. Simply singing inspiring songs, praying loud prayers, and having great men and women of God lay hands on them were not going to do it. They had to obey the voice of the Lord.

Here is another passage:

"Come now, and let us reason together, saith the LORD: though your sins be as scarlet, they shall be as white as snow; though they be red like crimson, they shall be as wool. If ye be willing and obedient, ye shall eat the good of the land" (Is. 1:18-19).

Make it Happen!

According to the beautiful passage above, in order to experience the fulfillment of the promises to be as "white as snow" and "as wool" and to "eat the good of the land," one has to "reason together" with the Lord and "be willing and obedient." The conditions have no exceptions! Those who want to enjoy the promises in the passage must qualify by meeting the conditions.

Here is another passage:

"My son, if thou wilt receive my words, and hide my commandments with thee; So that thou incline thine ear unto wisdom, and apply thine heart to understanding; Yea, if thou criest after knowledge, and liftest up thy voice for understanding; If thou seekest her as silver, and searchest for her as for hid treasures; Then shalt thou understand the fear of the LORD, and find the knowledge of God. For the LORD giveth wisdom: out of his mouth cometh knowledge and understanding" (Prov. 2:1–6).

In order to receive wisdom and walk in the fear of the Lord, the passage expects believers to meet some conditions. I guess you can identify the conditions: *"if thou criest after knowledge, and liftest up thy voice for understanding"* and *"searchest for her as for hid treasures."* Attentive readers can identify other conditions in the passage.

Based on the passage, wisdom belongs to those that qualify by meeting some conditions. The passage shows that those desiring wisdom must value it highly and seek knowledge and understanding with the commitment, determination, and dedication that people have when they seek hidden treasures. They must open their ears and hearts to wisdom, understand the fear of the Lord, and apply wisdom to their lives.

Here is another passage. Pay attention to the conditions:

"Praise ye the LORD. Blessed is the man that feareth the LORD, that delighteth greatly in his commandments. His seed shall be mighty upon earth: the generation of the upright shall be blessed. Wealth and riches shall be in his house: and his righteousness endureth for ever" (Ps. 112:1-3)

The blessings in the above passage belong to those that fear the Lord and delight greatly in His commandments. The blessings are for the upright.

David understood the concept of qualification when he instructed his son Solomon about nurturing a healthy relationship with God and building the temple. Here is portion from his charge to Solomon:

"And thou, Solomon my son, know thou the God of thy father, and serve him with a perfect heart and with a willing mind: for the LORD searcheth all hearts, and understandeth all the imaginations of the thoughts: if thou seek him, he will be found of thee; but if thou forsake him, he will cast thee off for ever. Take heed now; for the LORD hath chosen thee to build an house for the sanctuary: be strong, and do it" (1 Chron. 28:9-10).

He knew that God chose Solomon to build the temple. However, he also understood that Solomon needed to seek God and walk in His ways in order for him to

Make it Happen!

fulfill the plan of God. The fact that God chose Solomon to build the temple did not guarantee that Solomon would actually build it. Solomon needed to behave righteously and live on God's terms.

Read these verses in the passage below to see the qualifications for the promises in them:

"The righteous shall flourish like the palm tree: he shall grow like a cedar in Lebanon. Those that be planted in the house of the LORD shall flourish in the courts of our God" (Ps. 92:12–13).

As you may have noticed, the promise in the passage is for the righteous people who are "planted" in the house of the Lord.

Can you identify the conditions in the promises below?

"The hand of the diligent shall bear rule: but the slothful shall be under tribute" (Prov. 12:24).

"Seest thou a man diligent in his business? he shall stand before kings; he shall not stand before mean men" (Prov. 22:29).

"A wise servant shall have rule over a son that causeth shame, and shall have part of the inheritance among the brethren" (Prov. 17:2).

"The king's favour is toward a wise servant: but his wrath is against him that causeth shame"
(Prov. 14:35).

"Blessed is the man that walketh not in the counsel of the ungodly, nor standeth in the way of sinners, nor sitteth in the seat of the scornful. But his delight is in the law of the LORD; and in his law doth he meditate day and night. And he shall be like a tree planted by the rivers of water, that bringeth forth his fruit in his season; his leaf also shall not wither; and whatsoever he doeth shall prosper" (Ps. 1:1–3).

Some people may say, "Well, that was back then in the Old Testament. We are now living in the New Testament and in the time of grace. Jesus has already paid the price for our blessings."

Such people are making a serious mistake. The fact is that principles do not change with time. They stand for generations and outlive dispensations. The New Testament did not put an end to the principle of qualification.

Read the following Bible passages in the New Testament and see if you can notice the conditions attached to them:

"Not every one that saith unto me, Lord, Lord, shall enter into the kingdom of heaven; but he that doeth the will of my Father which is in heaven. Many will say to me in that day, Lord, Lord, have we not prophesied in thy name? and in thy name have cast out devils? and in thy name done many wonderful works? And then will I profess unto them, I never knew you: depart from me, ye that work iniquity. Therefore whosoever heareth these sayings of mine, and doeth them, I will liken him unto a wise man, which built his house upon a rock: And the rain descended, and the floods came, and the winds blew,

and beat upon that house; and it fell not: for it was founded upon a rock" (Matt. 7:21–25).

The Lord Jesus Christ is saying here that it takes more than calling Him "Lord" to enter into the kingdom of heaven. He presented the qualification as *"he that doeth the will of my Father which is in heaven"* (Matt. 7:21).

Here is another passage:

"And these signs shall follow them that believe; In my name shall they cast out devils; they shall speak with new tongues; They shall take up serpents; and if they drink any deadly thing, it shall not hurt them; they shall lay hands on the sick, and they shall recover" (Mark 16:17–18).

The passage says that signs will follow *"them that believe."*

Here is another one:

"But he that shall endure unto the end, the same shall be saved" (Matt. 24:13).

Here are more Bible passages outlining this concept:

"Even as Abraham believed God, and it was accounted to him for righteousness. Know ye therefore that they which are of faith, the same are the children of Abraham" (Gal. 3:6–7).

The passage shows that Abraham's children are those that walk in faith.

"They answered and said unto him, Abraham is our father. Jesus saith unto them, If ye were Abraham's children, ye would do the works of Abraham. But now ye seek to kill me, a man that hath told you the truth, which I have heard of God: this did not Abraham" (John 8:39-40).

Abraham's children are those that do the works of Abraham.

Here are more passages confirming the principle of qualification in the New Testament. Can you identify the conditions for the fulfillment of the promises in these verses?

"Study to shew thyself approved unto God, a workman that needeth not to be ashamed, rightly dividing the word of truth" (2 Tim. 2:15).

"Let no man despise thy youth; but be thou an example of the believers, in word, in conversation, in charity, in spirit, in faith, in purity" (1 Tim. 4:12).

"And let us not be weary in well doing: for in due season we shall reap, if we faint not" (Gal. 6:9).

"But whoso looketh into the perfect law of liberty, and continueth therein, he being not a forgetful hearer, but a doer of the work, this man shall be blessed in his deed" (James 1:25).

Make it Happen!

What price are you willing to pay?

Shortly before His death, the Lord Jesus Christ called His disciples aside and began to talk to them about His imminent betrayal, death, and resurrection:

"Behold, we go up to Jerusalem; and the Son of man shall be betrayed unto the chief priests and unto the scribes, and they shall condemn him to death, And shall deliver him to the Gentiles to mock, and to scourge, and to crucify him: and the third day he shall rise again" (Matt. 20:18-19).

On hearing this, the sons of Zebedee worked out a plan towards securing prominent positions in the Kingdom. They took their mother along with them to the Master to present their special request. Read the passage below to see their requests:

"Then came to him the mother of Zebedee's children with her sons, worshipping him, and desiring a certain thing of him. And he said unto her, What wilt thou? She saith unto him, Grant that these my two sons may sit, the one on thy right hand, and the other on the left, in thy kingdom. But Jesus answered and said, Ye know not what ye ask. Are ye able to drink of the cup that I shall drink of, and to be baptized with the baptism that I am baptized with? They say unto him, We are able" (Matt. 20:20-22).

By asking them "Are you able to drink of the cup that I shall drink of and be baptized with the baptism that I am baptized with?" the Lord was asking if they were willing to die his kind of death. He was trying to make it clear to them that their ambition for sitting next to

Him in the Kingdom necessitates their readiness to pay the ultimate price.

"And when he had called the people unto him with his disciples also, he said unto them, Whosoever will come after me, let him deny himself, and take up his cross, and follow me" (Mark 8:34).

The willingness to pay the price is part of the requirements for reaching exceptional goals in life and in the Kingdom of God.

Ambitions Require Qualifications

Everyone may desire to be an elder or a bishop in the church, but becoming one requires meeting some conditions:

"This is a true saying, if a man desire the office of a bishop, he desireth a good work. A bishop then must be blameless, the husband of one wife, vigilant, sober, of good behaviour, given to hospitality, apt to teach; Not given to wine, no striker, not greedy of filthy lucre; but patient, not a brawler, not covetous; One that ruleth well his own house, having his children in subjection with all gravity; (For if a man know not how to rule his own house, how shall he take care of the church of God?) Not a novice, lest being lifted up with pride he fall into the condemnation of the devil. Moreover he must have a good report of them which are without; lest he fall into reproach and the snare of the devil" (1 Tim. 3:1–7).

To reach greater goals, pay more attention to the importance of qualification.

Make it Happen!

5. FIGHTERS ACHIEVE MORE IN LIFE!

"And the children of Joseph spake unto Joshua, saying, Why hast thou given me but one lot and one portion to inherit, seeing I am a great people, forasmuch as the LORD hath blessed me hitherto?" (Josh. 17:14).

Joshua succeeded Moses in the wilderness as the new leader of the children of Israel. One of Joshua's greatest tasks was to distribute lands to the people. Our opening passage shows the dissatisfaction of the children of Joseph with the portion that Joshua gave to them. They wanted to have more land.

The response of Joshua to their demand has some important lessons for believers eager to achieve greater goals in this world. We shall study their request more closely in a moment, but first, let us look at the background of the opening passage.

Understanding the background will help us to understand the situation better. Here is the first verse:

"There was also a lot for the tribe of Manasseh; for he was the firstborn of Joseph; to wit, for Machir the firstborn of Manasseh, the father of Gilead: because he

was a man of war, therefore he had Gilead and Bashan" (Josh. 17:1).

The verse above partially describes how Joshua gave lands to the descendants of Joseph.

Bible students know that Joseph had two sons: Manasseh and Ephraim. This verse mentions the children of Manasseh in general and Machir, the first born of Manasseh, in particular.

The children of Manasseh in general received *"a lot"* for one reason, namely, because they were the firstborn of Joseph. That was their only qualification.

However, Machir, the firstborn of Manasseh, received Gilead and Bashan because *"he was a man of war."*

Machir was not only a descendant of Joseph. He had an additional qualification and a reputation as a warrior or a fighter, and Joshua recognized this by giving him Gilead and Bashan.

We saw the principle of qualification in the previous chapter of this book, and we see Joshua applying the principle here by honoring the qualification of Machir.

Inheritance versus Achievement

At this point, we need to understand two more things before we proceed with the chapter. They are Inheritance and Achievement.

1. ***Inheritance:*** Put simply, an inheritance is that which a person gets by succession or heredity. It is usually the result of the efforts of someone else. For example, a man may build a great house and leave it for his son when he dies. The son may know nothing about building a house, and he may not have money to build a house of his own, but he can become a house owner following the death of his father.

One may simply qualify for inheritance based on blood relationship to someone that has something to transfer. In this way, the child of a rich and successful person can receive riches and success through the efforts of his father, even though the child may be lazy and stupid!

While relationship may qualify a person to inherit wealth in this way, such a person must have other qualities or qualifications in order to keep, grow, and multiply the wealth for the next generation.

2. ***Achievement:*** An achievement is something that someone has succeeded in doing. It is the result of a person's conscious efforts. To achieve, one must learn principles, follow principles, learn the trade, study intensely, make the right decisions, and manage time, money, energy, and so on. An achiever cannot afford to be careless, lazy, and stupid.

While an inheritance may give someone a head start, one must be an achiever to succeed in times of challenges and to preserve valuable inheritance for many generations. An inheritance speaks of the wisdom, the hard work, and the success of those that went ahead of you. Achievement speaks of your own success and the result of your own effort.

God left His children in this world with inheritances in order to help them move faster ahead and achieve greatness for His glory. He left us here to be achievers so that we could in turn leave inheritances for other people.

Achievers make things happen. They identify values, set goals, work on their character, and press forward with healthy attitudes to fulfill their dreams and accomplish their missions in life.

Portions for Machir, the Son of Manasseh

With the above in mind, let us now take a closer look at the first verse:

"There was also a lot for the tribe of Manasseh; for he was the firstborn of Joseph; to wit, for Machir the firstborn of Manasseh, the father of Gilead: because he was a man of war, therefore he had Gilead and Bashan" (Josh. 17:1).

As we have noted, the tribe of Manasseh received a lot simply because Manasseh was the firstborn of Joseph. That was their only qualification. They received the blessing through inheritance. This was a simple qualification. They did not need to make it happen. It simply happened to them.

Many basic privileges of life require simple qualifications. For example, many people are citizens of countries because they were born in such countries. Being born there was their only qualification. It is not a person's achievement to be born in a particular location, but being of certain nationalities can come with privileges and rights as well as with responsibilities.

Foreigners normally need work permits and residence permits, and they must meet strict requirements in order to live and work in such countries; but citizens, by virtue of their constitutional rights and privileges, do not have to go through the trouble of obtaining such documents.

The verse shows that the tribe of Manasseh received their lot because of Joseph. Joseph inherited blessings because of his father, Jacob. Jacob inherited blessings because of his father, Isaac. Isaac inherited blessings because of his father, Abraham. Abraham received blessings because of his commitment to God. Abraham was the achiever that opened the door of blessings to the future generations of his children, so that Manasseh would benefit many generations later.

Some of the rich people in the world today are managing wealth created through the achievements of several generations of predecessors. Bearing certain surnames can open doors of great opportunities, while other surnames can close such doors.

Citizenship of certain countries commands respect abroad, while citizenship of some countries can increase scrutiny at border checkpoints. This can make the citizenship of one country more attractive than another to the frequent traveler.

The Lord Jesus Christ understood that the Jews, as descendants of Abraham, needed to have the privileges of experiencing the power of God through Him before extending such privileges to foreigners. We can see this through His encounter with a Greek woman:

"For a certain woman, whose young daughter had an unclean spirit, heard of him, and came and fell at his feet: The woman was a Greek, a Syrophenician by nation; and she besought him that he would cast forth the devil out of her daughter. But Jesus said unto her, Let the children first be filled: for it is not meet to take the children's bread, and to cast it unto the dogs. And she answered and said unto him, Yes, Lord: yet the dogs under the table eat of the children's crumbs. And he said unto her, For this saying go thy way; the devil is gone out of thy daughter. And when she was come to her house, she found the devil gone out, and her daughter laid upon the bed" (Mark 7:25–30).

The woman understood this principle too and refused to take offense at the Lord's words. On the contrary, she received the truth with humility and asked for the "crumbs," and she received her breakthrough. She had no priority or right by inheritance, but she obtained favor through insight in the subject matter and her attitude of humility and faith.

To receive some privileges, people may change their citizenship through the process of naturalization and become citizens of a country other than that of their birth.

While citizenship by birth may not be an achievement, citizenship through naturalization may be an achievement because of the strict conditions that foreigners must meet before qualifying for citizenship in attractive countries.

Special Places for Machir, the Man of War

While citizenship of a country may come with specific privileges, it does not automatically qualify one for all privileges.

Some privileges require additional qualifications in the form of formal education, appropriate job experiences, and positive recommendations from respectable references. In working, one must be faithful and productive in order to qualify for promotions. One must achieve certain goals in order to receive some titles and special honors. An academic Doctorate degree belongs to people who meet rigorous academic and research standards. The most special things of life belong to those who attain special qualifications.

In the first verse of the book of Joshua, chapter eleven, the Bible shows us that Joshua gave Machir, the firstborn of Manasseh, the additional land of Gilead and Bashan for a very interesting reason; namely, *"because he was a man of war"*!

Make it Happen!

Machir was not just like all of the other people. He was a fighter. He was an achiever. He knew how to make things happen!

To put the situation into historical context, we have to remember that giants lived in the land of Gilead before the children of Israel arrived there.

Giants lived there before the arrival of the children of Israel because the land was strategic and attractive, and giants were the strongest people back then. Strength determined possessions in those days. The most precious lands usually belonged to the strongest people.

That is why the twelve spies of Israel unanimously agreed on the fruitfulness of the land of Canaan. One example of the fruitfulness of the land was obvious in the fact that a single cluster of grape harvest required two men to carry because of the large size and heavy weight of the harvest:

"And they came unto the brook of Eshcol, and cut down from thence a branch with one cluster of grapes, and they bare it between two upon a staff; and they brought of the pomegranates, and of the figs. The place was called the brook Eshcol, because of the cluster of grapes which the children of Israel cut down from thence. And they returned from searching of the land after forty days. And they went and came to Moses, and to Aaron, and to all the congregation of the children of Israel, unto the wilderness of Paran, to Kadesh; and brought back word unto them, and unto all the congregation, and shewed them the fruit of the land. And they told him, and said, We came unto the land whither thou sentest us,

and surely it floweth with milk and honey; and this is the fruit of it" (Num. 13:23-27).

The spies also noticed the presence of giants, the children of Anak, in the fertile land. This led ten of the twelve spies to conclude that the inhabitants of the land were too strong for the children of Israel to defeat:

"The Amalekites dwell in the land of the south: and the Hittites, and the Jebusites, and the Amorites, dwell in the mountains: and the Canaanites dwell by the sea, and by the coast of Jordan. And Caleb stilled the people before Moses, and said, Let us go up at once, and possess it; for we are well able to overcome it. But the men that went up with him said, We be not able to go up against the people; for they are stronger than we" (Num. 13:29-31).

Notice that the Amorites are on the list in the passage above. We shall come back to this shortly as we look at the achievements of the children of Machir.

Although ten of the spies did not see the possibility of the children of Israel taking the lands, Joshua and Caleb felt that victory was possible with the help of God. They then tried to encourage the people to trust the Lord and take the land, but it was far easier for the crowd to believe the words of the ten spies than it was for them to receive the opinion of two spies.

"And they brought up an evil report of the land which they had searched unto the children of Israel, saying, The land, through which we have gone to search it, is a land that eateth up the inhabitants thereof; and all the people that we saw in it are men of a great stature. And

there we saw the giants, the sons of Anak, which come of the giants: and we were in our own sight as grasshoppers, and so we were in their sight" (Num. 13:32–33).

Filled with fear, the children of Israel did not go into battle at the time. The land theoretically belonged to them because of the promise that God made to their fathers, Abraham, Isaac, and Jacob, but inheritance alone was not enough at that stage. They needed to be strong in their minds, have faith in God, and be willing to fight, with God on their side.

The promise of God to their fathers opened the door for them, but they needed to have the right mindset to walk through the door. God may have a great plan for a person, but such plans may also require faith, dedication, and personal effort to succeed. People do not automatically succeed in life just because it is the will of God for them to succeed. As we have seen earlier, exceptional achievements and progress require us to cooperate with God.

The words of discouragement from the ten spies had deep negative effects on the congregation and kept that generation from entering the Promised Land. They doubted the love of God in the face of the report and felt that He delivered them from Egypt in order to destroy them.

"Notwithstanding ye would not go up, but rebelled against the commandment of the LORD your God: And ye murmured in your tents, and said, Because the LORD hated us, he hath brought us forth out of the land of Egypt, to deliver us into the hand of the Amorites, to

destroy us. Whither shall we go up? our brethren have discouraged our heart, saying, The people is greater and taller than we; the cities are great and walled up to heaven; and moreover we have seen the sons of the Anakims there" (Deut. 1:26–28).

Many believers assume that the will of God does not come with challenges and begin to doubt His love for them when they face tough situations. They allow circumstances to discourage them and listen to words that do not inspire them to move forward in life.

Such people hardly stand the test of time. You must be different. You must make up your mind to press forward in the midst of challenges and voices of discouragement. Remember that precious lands normally have "giants."

Now, let us get back to Machir.

Gilead was on a strategically high elevation and known for the mountain. In those days, when there were no fighter jets or remote-controlled drones, mountains were important for battles because being positioned on them gave strategic advantages in times of war. Being on top of the mountain allows one to see enemies approaching from afar, reducing the element of surprise that enemies normally use to win wars.

As we have seen from the description of the dwellers of the land when Moses sent out the twelve spies, the Amorites lived in the land before the arrival of the children of Israel. The children of Machir defeated the Amorites in the land, and Moses gave them the territory. Joshua only confirmed the decision that

Make it Happen!

Moses made in this case as we can read from the passage below:

"And the children of Machir the son of Manasseh went to Gilead, and took it, and dispossessed the Amorite which was in it. And Moses gave Gilead unto Machir the son of Manasseh; and he dwelt therein" (Num. 32:39–40).

It was proper to let Machir have the territories, not just because he earned it but also because it was strategically important to have warriors in charge of such territories in order to retain the land in the hands of the Children of Israel. The children of Machir were great fighters, and Moses and Joshua knew that the land would be safer in their hands.

Bashan was also a valuable land. Historically, the area had soft soil, highly suitable for agriculture. In a time when people depended mainly on agriculture to survive, it was common for nations to fight over the possession of fertile lands. Bashan was such a desirable land.

The second verse of Joshua, chapter 17, says:

"There was also a lot for the rest of the children of Manasseh by their families..." (Josh. 17:2).

There was a portion for the "rest" of the people. Achievers do not like to be part of "the rest" of the people. They understand that they are unique and special, and they leave their mark on history.

The children of Joseph needed more than deep desires!

Let us now return to the opening passage of this chapter:

"And the children of Joseph spake unto Joshua, saying, Why hast thou given me but one lot and one portion to inherit, seeing I am a great people, forasmuch as the LORD hath blessed me hitherto?" (Josh. 17:14).

After receiving their lot from Joshua, the rest of the children of Joseph soon began to feel that they deserved more lands, and they could not wait to express their dissatisfaction to Joshua:

"Why hast thou given me but one lot and one portion to inherit?" they asked.

They felt that they deserved more, and they stated two reasons for such a feeling:

(1) *"I am a great people."*
(2) *"The LORD hath blessed me."*

Feeling great and blessed, they realized that God must have more in store for them. They could no longer feel comfortable with the status quo. Something needed to change! They could not afford to settle for less.

Whenever God wants to promote people, He gives them a feeling of dissatisfaction with the status quo. They then begin to feel that there has to be more to life than the life that they have been living. They soon begin to feel left behind. They will no longer feel proud of their existing achievements.

Something deep within them tells them that they can do more and that they need to do more. Some of them will begin to see the needs around them and feel dissatisfied with their income. They will feel that they need to make more money so that they can touch more lives. They will grow in their sense of responsibilities and desire to do more for their world and for God.

Such people will develop a strong desire to move forward to reach greater goals and to break existing records. It is then common for the ignorant world around them to brand them as "arrogant," "unthankful," "ambitious," "unrealistic," and so on, but deep within, they feel a force pulling on them to move up higher and to go further.

They stay up late at night thinking about greater goals, and their minds are preoccupied during the day with the need to realize their full potential. This is one of the ways that God works within people to move them forward in life.

The Bible says:

"For it is God which worketh in you both to will and to do of his good pleasure" (Phil. 2:13).

"Now in the first year of Cyrus king of Persia, that the word of the LORD by the mouth of Jeremiah might be fulfilled, the LORD stirred up the spirit of Cyrus king of Persia, that he made a proclamation throughout all his kingdom, and put it also in writing..." (Ezra 1:1).

"Then rose up the chief of the fathers of Judah and Benjamin, and the priests, and the Levites, with all them whose spirit God had raised, to go up to build the house of the LORD which is in Jerusalem" (Ezra 1:5).

"Thy people shall be willing in the day of thy power, in the beauties of holiness from the womb of the morning: thou hast the dew of thy youth" (Ps. 110:3).

"The king's heart is in the hand of the LORD, as the rivers of water: he turneth it whithersoever he will" (Prov. 21:1).

With a strong desire for a bigger portion, the sons of Joseph went to Joshua expecting him to give them more lands. They felt special and more deserving. They felt that they belonged on a higher level, in larger territories.

Feeling special in their case was not an exaggeration. They were special indeed. Their father, Joseph, was the reason why the rest of the tribes survived. He was a Prime Minister in Egypt in a time of great famine, and God used him to get the rest of the children of Israel into the country.

The children of Joseph could be proud of their father. He was a blessed man. They were now conscious of their great heritage and could no longer settle for less.

Joshua did not rebuke them for being "ambitious" and "ungrateful." On the contrary, he was happy to see that they were thinking bigger. He actually agreed with them that it was okay for the tribe to have more property.

He then showed them the possibilities of getting more land and encouraged them to make it happen.

"And Joshua answered them, If thou be a great people, then get thee up to the wood country, and cut down for thyself there in the land of the Perizzites and of the giants, if mount Ephraim be too narrow for thee" (Josh. 17:15).

Joshua gave them the portion that was available for normal inheritance. However, there were still lands available for warriors! They looked up to Joshua to help fulfill their dreams, but he made it clear that the next level of their expansion was in their own hands.

Trainers, pastors, parents, politicians, employers, friends, and family members may be able to help you with certain things in life, but you must put in personal effort if you want to fully realize the greatest dreams burning within your spirit. Achievers take responsibilities for their own progress and take steps towards the realization of their worthy goals.

Dreamers not willing to fight the battles necessary for their success can only live in fantasies. Such people do not achieve impressive goals. You must be different.

Serious visionaries cannot afford to allow fear or circumstances stop them from pursuing the plan of God for their lives. Dreamers run into battles when others are fleeing. They hold on when others give up and stand strong when others faint.

The children of Joseph felt the need to expand but soon began to doubt their greatness as they considered the giants in the land:

"And the children of Joseph said, The hill is not enough for us: and all the Canaanites that dwell in the land of the valley have chariots of iron, both they who are of Bethshean and her towns, and they who are of the valley of Jezreel" (Jos 17:16).

They could not see themselves defeating a well-armed army of giants notorious for their strong chariots of iron.

It is quite common for people to hesitate about pursuing their dreams when they focus on the often-intimidating challenges and costs of realizing those dreams.

Are the challenges of your dreams intimidating you too? Do not give up! Let the words of Joshua to the children of Joseph encourage you:

"And Joshua spake unto the house of Joseph, even to Ephraim and to Manasseh, saying, Thou art a great people, and hast great power: thou shalt not have one lot only: But the mountain shall be thine; for it is a wood, and thou shalt cut it down: and the outgoings of it shall be thine: for thou shalt drive out the Canaanites, though they have iron chariots, and though they be strong" (Jos 17:17-18).

Many people want the greater and better things of life and hope to have such things delivered to them by the efforts of others. They forget that such things require their own personal commitments.

Anyone who wants to excel in the will of God must be willing to pay the price for progress. Achievers do not expect success delivered to them on a silver plate. They take conscious steps to make things happen and to achieve success. If you want to move beyond your present level, then consider your role in making progress, and plan to make the necessary contributions.

We live in a fighter's world, period!

As we have seen in this chapter, it takes dedicated fighters to possess the mountains and the special lands with the most precious things of life. It takes fighters to press forward in tough times and to overcome challenges and reach exceptional goals.

God wants you to live for His glory. This will require you to reach goals beyond the average person around you. The path to reaching such extraordinary goals is often full of obstacles, opposition, and many challenges. You will need to be strong in your mind, courageous with your attitude, stable in your character, wise and strategic with your approach, and consistent in your commitment in order to reach such goals.

Great ideas usually generate skepticism and raise doubts in the minds of average people. Others may not see what you see in the vision that you want to accomplish, until they begin to see the fruits of your efforts. In the eyes of the average person, that great dream of yours may only make you look ambitious, proud, and arrogant.

Do not expect motivation from people who are not seeing as you see and do not believe as you believe. Therefore, it should not sound strange to you if they try to discourage you. Some of them have good intentions. They want to save you the headache, protect you from wasting your money, and prevent you from failing and paying a high price in the process. They care about you and want to see you play it safe in life. They are not necessarily your enemies. They are just friends that do not see as you see at the time that you want them to stand with you.

Therefore, you need to be willing to stand alone when necessary and to do your part. Do not share your dreams with everyone. Be selective about the people that you confide in. Your world will be watching.

Some are ready to copy you when you succeed. Others are waiting to see you fail so that they can say, "You see, I knew it, and I saw it coming. I was sure that the idea was doomed to fail, and you see, I was right." Others are watching to see you succeed so that they can be proud and say that they know someone special. A relatively few people will be willing to stand with you and give you the moral, spiritual, and material support that you need.

Lack of support may slow down the progress of achievers, but achievers are normally resilient, and they know how to defy the odds. They usually succeed eventually because they never give up! They are fighters!

There are portions in life for exceptional people, and there are portions in life for the rest of the people. If you are having exceptional dreams and there are great ideas burning within you, then you must make up your mind to be a fighter. You must decide to make those dreams come true. You have to be an achiever, one that overcomes limitations and makes things happen!

We live in a fighter's world. The world of progress and greater achievement belongs to those who are willing to take up challenges. Such people control commerce, influence policies, and set the standard in fashion, entertainment, sports, and the environment. Fighters lead their trade. They launch new ideas and create their own opportunities with the help of God. Fighters are strong in their minds and in their emotions.

They get up if they fall! They can boldly declare,

"Rejoice not against me, O mine enemy: when I fall, I shall arise; when I sit in darkness, the LORD shall be a light unto me" (Mic. 7:8).

Paul wrote to Timothy:

"Thou therefore endure hardness, as a good soldier of Jesus Christ" (2 Tim. 2:3).

"But watch thou in all things, endure afflictions, do the work of an evangelist, make full proof of thy ministry" (2 Tim. 4:5).

He was telling him to be tough!

The Lord instructed Joshua to be strong and to take the men of war with him in order to possess the land of Ai.

"And the LORD said unto Joshua, Fear not, neither be thou dismayed: take all the people of war with thee, and arise, go up to Ai: see, I have given into thy hand the king of Ai, and his people, and his city, and his land" (Josh. 8:1).

The Lord Jesus Christ said:

"And from the days of John the Baptist until now the kingdom of heaven suffereth violence, and the violent take it by force" (Matt. 11:12).

Be ready for all situations!

Some people think that Christianity equals timidity, but this is wrong. There is a time and place for everything and for every personality!

Many believers know the names of God according to His personality, character, deeds, and promises. For example, we call Him *Jehovah-Jireh*, our *Provider*; *Jehovah Shalom*, our *Peace*; *Jehovah Tsidkenu*, our *Righteousness*; and so on.

We know that He is God to us in different ways, and at different times, depending on our needs and on the situation at hand. Many people forget that believers must also show different character traits according to the need of their situation. We must be adaptable without compromising our spiritual stand.

Here are some of the characteristics that God expects of His children, in no particular order:

The Lord Jesus said, *"Behold, I send you forth as sheep in the midst of wolves: be ye therefore wise as serpents, and harmless as doves"* (Matt. 10:16).

1. **Serpent:** This means that we need to be smart like serpents. People should not be able to fool us.

2. **Dove:** This means that we have to be careful enough to avoid hurting people. This means that people should be safe with us.

3. **Sheep:** This means that we are to submit to the leadership of the Master and obey the voice of the Good Shepherd in all that we do in this world.

The Bible declares:

"The wicked flee when no man pursueth: but the righteous are bold as a lion" (Prov. 28:1).

4. **Lion:** This means that those living right are bold. The lion is bold and difficult to push around. God's children need to have and demonstrate this quality.

Paul the Apostle encouraged Timothy to endure hardness as a soldier:

"Thou therefore endure hardness, as a good soldier of Jesus Christ (2 Tim. 2:3).

5. **Soldier:** This means that we need to be strong in the midst of challenges and live our lives with courage, discipline, and unstoppable resolve, irrespective of the conditions on the ground.

The Lord Jesus said:

"Blessed are the peacemakers: for they shall be called the children of God" (Matt. 5:9).

6. **Children:** This means that we are to live like our Heavenly Father, in the spirit of true love, ceasing opportunities in order to promote and ensure peace.

The Bible says:

"As every man hath received the gift, even so minister the same one to another, as good stewards of the manifold grace of God" (1 Pet. 4:10).

"Let a man so account of us, as of the ministers of Christ, and stewards of the mysteries of God. Moreover it is required in stewards, that a man be found faithful" (1 Cor. 4:1–2).

7. **Stewards:** This means that we need to be faithful, trustworthy, and reliable.

Make it Happen!

"Unto the church of God which is at Corinth, to them that are sanctified in Christ Jesus, called to be saints, with all that in every place call upon the name of Jesus Christ our Lord, both theirs and ours" (1 Cor. 1:2).

    8. Saints: This requires us to walk in purity as people set aside to live according to God's moral and spiritual standard.

"Now then we are ambassadors for Christ, as though God did beseech you by us: we pray you in Christ's stead, be ye reconciled to God" (2 Cor. 5:20).

    9. Ambassador: This means that we are to live as representatives of Heaven, furthering the interests of the Kingdom of God in our world. We are to represent the Kingdom honorably and admirably, making the Kingdom attractive to our world in all that we do.

The Lord Jesus Christ told His disciples...

"Ye are the light of the world. A city that is set on an hill cannot be hid. Neither do men light a candle, and put it under a bushel, but on a candlestick; and it giveth light unto all that are in the house. Let your light so shine before men, that they may see your good works, and glorify your Father which is in heaven" (Matt. 5:14–16).

    10. Light of the world: This means that we are to do good works for the world to see. This is useful when we see people in need. We are to feed the hungry, give shelter to the homeless, clothe the naked, and take care of those in need of help.

Some people are of the opinion that believers are to be sheep. Others believe that they are to be like doves. There are also those that feel that true believers have to be lions. The true character of true believers continues to be the subject of intense debate around the world.

However, to excel in life, believers must behave according to the word of God. This means being all of the above, and more, according to the needs of the time. Being a "dove" when one should be a "lion" can result in timidity and fear in the face of challenges. Being a "lion" when one should be a "dove" can intimidate and hurt the feelings of innocent people.

Fighters in Different Ways

Fighting does not always mean physical aggression or violence. To fight also means to contend as in a contest, to defeat opposition, to take on obstacles, and to resist aggression or violence. It means to set aside excuses for failure and to take on challenges. In physical battles, such as in a time of war, fighting normally involves physical weapons and aggression.

The path to prosperity often involves emotional, spiritual, and mental obstacles. As a result, the determined achiever must have the mental, emotional, and spiritual strength necessary to win and to move forward.

Sometimes to fight means doing everything possible to be a dove. Sometimes it means doing what it takes to be a lion. Fighting can mean being the light of the

Make it Happen!

world in a time and place where that is extremely difficult. God wants His children to be strong!

"Finally, my brethren, be strong in the Lord, and in the power of his might" (Eph. 6:10).

Fighters set excuses aside and move forward. They learn to overcome their weaknesses, build on their strengths, focus on their goals, and move forward.

Make up your mind to be the achiever that God wants you to be.

6. MAKE IT HAPPEN!

"Neglect not the gift that is in thee, which was given thee by prophecy, with the laying on of the hands of the presbytery. Meditate upon these things; give thyself wholly to them; that thy profiting may appear to all. Take heed unto thyself, and unto the doctrine; continue in them: for in doing this thou shalt both save thyself, and them that hear thee" (1 Tim. 4:14–16).

Our opening passage in this chapter is a portion from Paul's letter to Timothy, a young man whom the Apostle left in charge of the church in Ephesus. Timothy had to lead a congregation with people older than him and was naturally insecure. However, the Apostle believed in this young man, and we can tell from Paul's instructions that he wanted Timothy to succeed.

The instructions in the passage above contain essential keys for progress and greater achievements in life. Let us look at the passage more closely and break down the content to see the lessons that we can learn.

1. *"Neglect not the gift that is in thee":* This is a call to pay attention to the gifts in the life of Timothy. A gift is a special endowment that

allows a person to accomplish or to do certain things with relative ease. Such a person thrives in the areas of the gifts where others must struggle.

There are gifted speakers, writers, singers, instrumentalists, athletes, and so on in our world today, making media headlines and impressing our world. To excel in life, you need to recognize your gifts and appreciate them. Many people neglect their gifts because they feel that the gifts of other people are superior to theirs.

They then try to emulate the gifts of other people and end up working harder than necessary while getting inferior results. God made us unique so that we can make different kinds of contributions to our world. Every gift is essential and important.

One person can make a million dollars playing basketball. Another person can make a million dollars as a cleaner.

To many people, the idea of making a million dollars as a cleaner sounds difficult to believe because cleaners are among the lowest paid people in the world today. However, a passionate cleaner can excel, set up a cleaning company, grow it into a global cleaning franchise, and generate millions of dollars annually.

People who appreciate their gifts can become great achievers in their fields. Do not neglect the gifts in your life.

2. ***"...which was given thee by prophecy, with the laying on of the hands of the presbytery"***: Paul was referring to the gifts that Timothy received through prophecy and the laying on of the hands of the elders in the church. Some people have innate gifts that were present from the time they were in their mother's womb. Others receive gifts through prayers and words from God's anointed servants.

A gift that was not part of your life at birth may begin to manifest in your life after some spiritual experiences or prayers. The laying on of hands may transfer power, virtue, and gifts. Therefore, pay close attention to any special interests that you begin to have after a spiritual experience.

3. ***"Meditate upon these things":*** Paul is asking Timothy here to invest quality time in thinking about these things. To meditate means to spend quality time thinking about something. Great achievers are great thinkers. You must make time to think if you want to succeed. We live in a time when people are too busy to think. They are constantly on the move, doing one thing or the other and living on hindsight wisdom.

Make time to think about what you can do with your gifts. Ask yourself questions about the potential in your life. How can you take your gift to the next level? Whom can you serve with your gift? Where do people need your gift the most? Where are people more likely to appreciate and pay more for your services?

Make it Happen!

What must you do to help your world notice the services that you can render? What kind of business can you build around your gift? How can you serve the Kingdom of God and your world with your gift? How do you plan to stay humble and faithful to God when you succeed? How do you intend to reward those that help you along the way?

How soon do you want to start touching your world? How do you start with your current resources and in your present situation? What steps can you take today to move closer to your great goals? Make time to meditate, and you will excel!

> 4. *"... give thyself wholly to them...":* This expression means to give oneself completely to something without reservations. It means to invest the time, energy, money, attention, and other resources necessary to explore, develop, grow, and capitalize on something. It means to hone the skills, refine the gift, and become a master, expert, or leader in it.

Paul did not want Timothy to treat his gifts casually, like a hobby. He expected Timothy to perfect the gifts like a superior designer, a specialist, and one that is determined to make major impacts with such gifts.

Give yourself wholly to the purpose of God for your gifts. Do not settle for anything less than all that you can do. Be critical with yourself about your performance, and learn to beat your past records each time. Get trainers, mentors, and advisers when necessary.

Listen to critical evaluations, and improve in your knowledge. Make your performance wow the professional world, and then move on to beat that record. Do not stop short of making your Heavenly Father proud. Practice when others are wasting their time and their lives. Work with passion and dedication.

> 5. ***"… that thy profiting may appear to all…:*** This phrase means to have visible or tangible benefits. In essence, Paul was telling Timothy that people around him should be able to see his effectiveness. The Lord Jesus Christ told His disciples to let their light shine for people to see.

The world around you needs to see your progress, your usefulness, your effectiveness, and your impact. Paul did not want Timothy's progress to be a secret matter. He wanted his progress to be visible. He also did not want Timothy to remain on the same level unnecessarily for too long. He wanted the young man to progress and excel.

God wants you to prosper in everything that you do, and He wants others to see you prosper.

> 6. ***"Take heed unto thyself":*** This is another way of saying "pay attention to you." In other words, make sure that you are doing okay. Many people develop their gifts but fail to develop their character. They succeed professionally but fail personally and privately. They are celebrities in their world but are junkies behind the scenes. God wants you to be okay.

Make it Happen!

Paul wanted Timothy to pay attention to his own life. Learn to be fit, spiritually, mentally, physically, morally, emotionally, and otherwise. The gifts in your life depend on you to thrive. Therefore, you are very important.

God expects you to love your neighbor as you love yourself. This is only possible if you know how to love yourself. You have to love yourself and then love your neighbor in the same way. Stay away from anything that can pollute your spirit, mind, and body.

Be honest with yourself. Do not live a life behind the scenes that you are not proud to live in the open. Never deceive yourself. Stay away from hypocrisy, and be true to the life that you profess.

7. *"... and unto the doctrine..."*: In addition to paying attention to himself, Paul also instructed Timothy to pay attention to the doctrine. A doctrine is a standard teaching, creed, dogma, or principle. It is a person's stand on a subject or matter. It is the belief that keeps a person doing certain things, staying away from some things, and saying "yes" or "no" to situations.

Paul was calling on Timothy to be a man of principle, a person living by a high moral standard. To excel in your world and see great things happen through your life, you must learn principles and live by them. Do not simply follow the crowd. You must dare to be different!

Great achievers live by principles and have the courage to stand for what they believe. They do not just bow to the crowd. They do not allow the masses to corrupt their minds.

8. ***"... continue in them...":*** To continue in something means to focus and be consistent in it. Some people have the habit of starting up things with passion and enthusiasm only to abandon them when the process gets tougher. Achievers pursue their goals consistently, improving along the way, and never giving up! Paul wanted Timothy to be steadfast and consistent. Continue to do the right things, steadily, no matter how long the journey may take you.

9. ***"... for in doing this thou shalt both save thyself...":*** The word "save" in the verse means to deliver, protect, preserve, or heal. Developing the gifts, exercising the gifts, and continuing in the doctrines were going to benefit Timothy, and Paul wanted him to know that.

Many professional athletes today make their livelihood from their gifts and passion. They literally preserve their lives and the lives of their family members through their gifts. Many God-fearing people today walk in principles that preserve their lives in good health. We benefit from doing the right things.

10. ***"... and them that hear thee":*** Timothy had a position of influence, and the progress of several people depended on his life. His words had the potential to lead people in the right direction, but they also had the potential to

lead them in the wrong direction. Paul wanted him to realize that other people were depending on him.

In life, we influence people, and others influence us. We must live, think, and speak with the consciousness that others are looking up to us.

Someone, somewhere is waiting for you to make it happen!

Your progress can open the doors of progress to other people in your family, neighborhood, church, community, and school and in nations beyond your place of birth.

Your financial success can help to make the world a better place for many people in need of support.

You can be the reason why some children will no longer have to go to bed without food. Your new level of achievement can reduce the number of homeless people in our world. You may be the reason why someone on the way to Hell can now start heading to Heaven.

You can help to reduce the pain and the discouragement in many lives if you choose to pursue and perform the will of God for your life.

Your invention and innovation may make people work more efficiently and effortlessly. Your new business may create job opportunities for many. Those that you employ can use the income to take care of their families, give their children a quality education, and prepare leaders for tomorrow.

That book that you need to write may change the way that thousands and millions of people think and may end up providing the keys that they need for their next level of achievement. Someone, somewhere is waiting to read your book.

Someone, somewhere is waiting for you to set up the business. Someone, somewhere is waiting for you to make more money and become the "angel" in human form! People are waiting for you to make it happen!

God brought you to this world to leave your mark on it. He designed the gifts in your life to set you apart and make you different from the rest of the people around you. He is counting on you to capitalize on them for the establishment of His purpose in your life, and through you, for the benefit of a world in need and for the glory of His name.

Live to make God's purpose happen in your life!

One of our most important duties in life is to discover God's purpose for us in this life, identify His mandates for us at every stage of our lives, qualify for them, and take conscious steps to fulfill them.

People sometimes ask the question, "How do I know the will of God?" That is a subject of another book.

Make it Happen!

However, the following hints may help you start your search:

1. ***The needs keeping you up at night:*** Several people watched a documentary about the condition of orphans in a developing country. Most of them prayed and donated money but one of them had many sleepless nights thinking about the children and the need to give them special personal care. She went on to be a missionary in a far country, taking care of orphans. She believes that she is now doing the will of God for her life and she has found peace within herself.

Many entrepreneurs touching lives around the world today started their journeys with the needs of other people in mind. Most inventors wanted to make life easier for people. They all wanted people to have better goods and services, live more efficiently, and enjoy life better. They then built revenue streams to make money while serving, and became rich in the process.

What are the needs keeping you awake at night? You may need to seek God's purpose for you there in order to move forward and make it happen!

2. ***The things driving your passion:*** Passion manifests in several ways. It can show up in the form of deep inner longing, desire, hunger, or thirst. It can also show up in the form of anger. Passion can also be in the form of excitement. Passion does something deep within a person. Passion stirs up strong human emotions.

A passionate person can show anger against injustice and/or love for justice. A passionate person can show hatred for poverty and love for prosperity. Another person may show hatred for sickness and love for perfect health.

Different people are passionate about different things. Some people have a passion for fashion. Others are passionate about education. Others are passionate about business. Some people are passionate about politics. Others are passionate about ministry. Some people are passionate about health. Others are passionate about housing.

One may have a single main area of passion. It is also possible to have two or more areas of passion. What are you passionate about? The area(s) of your deepest passion may hint at the purpose of God for your life.

   3. *Your gifts:* The gifts and talents in your life may indicate the purpose of God for your life. He equips us from birth with the gifts that we need to do His purpose in our world. Therefore, we can observe the gifts in our lives and learn to understand why He is keeping us alive.

Once you identify the will of God for your life, pursue it, and live to perform it!

Follow the Lord's Example

The Lord Jesus Christ is our perfect example here. He studied the Scriptures to identify all of the prophecies about His life and then took specific steps to fulfill them. His focus in this life was to do the will of the Father. He worked consciously to live up to God's expectations.

He lived up to His full potential, wasting neither time nor resources. Read the Master's own words below, and you will notice that...

1. He lived with a sense of a higher purpose:

"For I came down from heaven, not to do mine own will, but the will of him that sent me" (John 6:38).

2. He found passion in doing the will of His Heavenly Father:

"Jesus saith unto them, My meat is to do the will of him that sent me, and to finish his work" (John 4:34).

3. He worked with a sense of urgency:

"I must work the works of him that sent me, while it is day: the night cometh, when no man can work" (John 9:4).

Many Christians today seem to be waiting endlessly for God to do things for them or for some other people to help take their lives to the next level. God wants us to take responsibility for our own progress and to take the initiative necessary to succeed in life. Once we know the right things to do, it becomes our duty to do them.

"Therefore to him that knoweth to do good, and doeth it not, to him it is sin" (James 4:17).

Accepting Responsibility

God created us to take responsibility. He placed Adam and Eve in charge of the Garden of Eden with responsibilities.

"And the LORD God took the man, and put him into the garden of Eden to dress it and to keep it" (Gen. 2:15).

God expected man to take care of the garden.

To be responsible means to be in charge, to be in control, to be accountable and as the one that must make the right things happen or prevent the wrong things from happening, depending on the situation. The person responsible is the one to blame for failures and the one worthy of praise for successes. To be responsible means to be answerable or liable. It means to have the power to determine the outcome of something.

God wants His children to take charge of their own lives and be fully responsible for their own progress.

Say "Goodbye" to Manna and "Hello" to Power!

The children of Israel were slaves in Egypt for hundreds of years, living in poverty because the

Make it Happen!

Egyptians oppressed them. With time, God delivered them through Moses and took care of them in the wilderness, where they received His instructions.

God fed them with Manna in the wilderness. Moses then handed over the leadership to Joshua, and he took them into the Promised Land, where they tilled the land, planted, and harvested through their efforts. Manna then stopped.

"And the manna ceased on the morrow after they had eaten of the old corn of the land; neither had the children of Israel manna any more; but they did eat of the fruit of the land of Canaan that year" (Josh. 5:12).

Pharaoh took care of them in Egypt when they were slaves. God took care of them in the wilderness when they were in His "school" and had no opportunities to work for their own food. However, when they entered the Promised Land, the fertile land, God made them responsible for their own progress. He expected them to work towards the fulfillment of His promises of abundance in their lives.

He did not only give them a fruitful land. He also gave them the abilities necessary to work on the land. In other words, He gave them power to work on the land for their own progress. Power is the ability to work or to make things happen. He empowered them to work on the land for bountiful harvest, to prosper and build houses, and to excel in all of their desires and in His will for their lives and for His glory.

Moses reminded them of this when he said...

"When thou hast eaten and art full, then thou shalt bless the LORD thy God for the good land which he hath given thee. Beware that thou forget not the LORD thy God, in not keeping his commandments, and his judgments, and his statutes, which I command thee this day: Lest when thou hast eaten and art full, and hast built goodly houses, and dwelt therein; And when thy herds and thy flocks multiply, and thy silver and thy gold is multiplied, and all that thou hast is multiplied; Then thine heart be lifted up, and thou forget the LORD thy God, which brought thee forth out of the land of Egypt, from the house of bondage; Who led thee through that great and terrible wilderness, wherein were fiery serpents, and scorpions, and drought, where there was no water; who brought thee forth water out of the rock of flint; Who fed thee in the wilderness with manna, which thy fathers knew not, that he might humble thee, and that he might prove thee, to do thee good at thy latter end; And thou say in thine heart, My power and the might of mine hand hath gotten me this wealth. But thou shalt remember the LORD thy God: for it is he that giveth thee power to get wealth, that he may establish his covenant which he sware unto thy fathers, as it is this day" (Deut. 8:10–18).

God gave them land, power, wisdom, and all of the abilities necessary for them to prosper in all of their ways and then left each one of them to determine their own levels of effectiveness based on their personal commitments to His principles and His goals for their lives. He was no longer directly responsible for their progress. He stopped giving them food and gave them the abilities, resources, and opportunities to cultivate their own food.

Make it Happen!

God removed the oppression of Egypt and the limitations of the Wilderness from their lives and left them with all that they needed for unlimited progress. With limitations lifted and opportunities abounding, it was now up to them to determine their own futures and the speed of their own progress. They had power to make things happen!

The world abounds with opportunities for anyone who will look in the right direction. The Bible contains powerful principles for anyone who wishes to progress in life. There are many educational opportunities for people who sincerely want to learn. Because of the wealth of wisdom that the Bible contains, God's children can prosper in this world beyond imagination, even without a single miracle or new supernatural act of God in our time.

Now add to that the special grace of God on their lives, the favor of God working with them, and the supernatural experiences that many of them experienced, and you will understand why God expects His children to lead and teach their world.

Having abilities comes with opportunities. If we can do something, and it is necessary to do, then God expects us to do it. Refusing to use our abilities because of laziness, fear, insecurity, and so on can lead to unnecessary failure, poverty, and lack.

The Bible says,

"The hand of the diligent shall bear rule: but the slothful shall be under tribute" (Prov. 12:24).

To be diligent means to be industrious or hardworking. The Bible is saying here that the industrious person will rule or be in charge while the lazy person will be under tribute. To be under tribute means to be a subject or under the rule of someone else.

"He also that is slothful in his work is brother to him that is a great waster" (Prov. 18:9).

This verse is saying that a lazy person is wasteful. Such a person wastes opportunities for harvest, opportunities for exploits, opportunities for progress, and so on.

"Let him that stole steal no more: but rather let him labour, working with his hands the thing which is good, that he may have to give to him that needeth" (Eph. 4:28).

God wants us to take on responsibilities, follow His instructions, and use our abilities to make things happen so that we can take care of ourselves and other people.

The Lord Jesus Christ made it happen!

Pay close attention to the life of the Lord Jesus Christ, and you will notice how He carefully studied the Scriptures to understand the predictions about His life and took specific conscious steps to make them happen. He understood that He was the Messiah, the Anointed One, and He understood that He had to live to fulfill the scriptures about His life.

Make it Happen!

Let us see some Bible passages to illustrate His conscious approach. As you read, pay attention to the phrase *"that it might be fulfilled."* The phrase means, *"in order to fulfill."*

"And he came and dwelt in a city called Nazareth: that it might be fulfilled which was spoken by the prophets, He shall be called a Nazarene" (Matt. 2:23).

"And leaving Nazareth, he came and dwelt in Capernaum, which is upon the sea coast, in the borders of Zabulon and Nephthalim: That it might be fulfilled which was spoken by Esaias the prophet, saying, The land of Zabulon, and the land of Nephthalim, by the way of the sea, beyond Jordan, Galilee of the Gentiles; The people which sat in darkness saw great light; and to them which sat in the region and shadow of death light is sprung up" (Matt. 4:13–16).

"When the even was come, they brought unto him many that were possessed with devils: and he cast out the spirits with his word, and healed all that were sick: That it might be fulfilled which was spoken by Esaias the prophet, saying, Himself took our infirmities, and bare our sicknesses"
(Matt. 8:16–17).

"Then the Pharisees went out, and held a council against him, how they might destroy him. But when Jesus knew it, he withdrew himself from thence: and great multitudes followed him, and he healed them all; And charged them that they should not make him known: That it might be fulfilled which was spoken by Esaias the prophet, saying, Behold my servant, whom I have

chosen; my beloved, in whom my soul is well pleased: I will put my spirit upon him, and he shall shew judgment to the Gentiles. He shall not strive, nor cry; neither shall any man hear his voice in the streets. A bruised reed shall he not break, and smoking flax shall he not quench, till he send forth judgment unto victory. And in his name shall the Gentiles trust" (Matt. 12:14-21).

"All these things spake Jesus unto the multitude in parables; and without a parable spake he not unto them: That it might be fulfilled which was spoken by the prophet, saying, I will open my mouth in parables; I will utter things which have been kept secret from the foundation of the world" (Matt. 13:34-35).

"And when they drew nigh unto Jerusalem, and were come to Bethphage, unto the mount of Olives, then sent Jesus two disciples, Saying unto them, Go into the village over against you, and straightway ye shall find an ass tied, and a colt with her: loose them, and bring them unto me. And if any man say ought unto you, ye shall say, The Lord hath need of them; and straightway he will send them. All this was done, that it might be fulfilled which was spoken by the prophet, saying, Tell ye the daughter of Sion, Behold, thy King cometh unto thee, meek, and sitting upon an ass, and a colt the foal of an ass" (Matt. 21:1-5).

"Now he that betrayed him gave them a sign, saying, Whomsoever I shall kiss, that same is he: hold him fast. And forthwith he came to Jesus, and said, Hail, master; and kissed him. And Jesus said unto him, Friend, wherefore art thou come? Then came they, and laid hands on Jesus, and took him. And, behold, one of them which were with Jesus stretched out his hand, and drew

his sword, and struck a servant of the high priest's, and smote off his ear. Then said Jesus unto him, Put up again thy sword into his place: for all they that take the sword shall perish with the sword. Thinkest thou that I cannot now pray to my Father, and he shall presently give me more than twelve legions of angels? But how then shall the scriptures be fulfilled, that thus it must be?" (Matt. 26:48–54).

He consciously took steps to fulfill the plan of the Father for His life by working towards the fulfillment of the promises about His life.

God expects us to pursue the dreams burning within us, to work on His vision and mandates, and to turn great ideas into realities. Will you make your Heavenly Father proud?

The Roles of Other People in Our Lives

Are we denying the fact that individuals are not always fully responsible for their own progress or failures in life? No! We are not denying this. The fact is that our progress may sometimes depend on the actions or inactions of certain people.

We shall look at this fact now and see that we can still decide to move forward and be successful in life, irrespective of adverse backgrounds and circumstances.

Let us face it! There are realistically stages in our lives when other people are responsible for our welfare and progress. For example, when we are children and too young to make decisions, our parents and guardians make decisions for us.

Parents and guardians normally have the first opportunities to protect children from danger and to teach them the fundamental principles of life. Children that receive proper foundations from home tend to have better chances of succeeding in life. Those that lack healthy upbringing tend to struggle more in life. Therefore, the challenges of many adults have their roots in the kind of preparations that their parents gave to them before they were able to make their own choices.

The Bible is aware of this fact and instructs parents to do the following:

"Train up a child in the way he should go: and when he is old, he will not depart from it" (Prov. 22:6).

"And, ye fathers, provoke not your children to wrath: but bring them up in the nurture and admonition of the Lord" (Eph. 6:4).

Growing up with the right leadership and under God-fearing parents certainly has advantages. Timothy had instructions from the Scriptures when he was growing up.

"And that from a child thou hast known the holy scriptures, which are able to make thee wise unto salvation through faith which is in Christ Jesus" (2 Tim. 3:15).

Make it Happen!

The Lord Jesus Christ also had effective parenting. His parents helped to fulfill some of the Scriptures about His life, preparing the way for Him to be effective and fruitful. God also helped to fulfill other parts.

The Bible passages below show the roles of God and the roles of Jesus' parents in the fulfillment of His destiny:

"And she shall bring forth a son, and thou shalt call his name JESUS: for he shall save his people from their sins. Now all this was done, that it might be fulfilled which was spoken of the Lord by the prophet." (Matt. 1:21–22).

"And being warned of God in a dream that they should not return to Herod, they departed into their own country another way. And when they were departed, behold, the angel of the Lord appeareth to Joseph in a dream, saying, Arise, and take the young child and his mother, and flee into Egypt, and be thou there until I bring thee word: for Herod will seek the young child to destroy him. When he arose, he took the young child and his mother by night, and departed into Egypt: And was there until the death of Herod: that it might be fulfilled which was spoken of the Lord by the prophet, saying, Out of Egypt have I called my son. Then Herod, when he saw that he was mocked of the wise men, was exceeding wroth, and sent forth, and slew all the children that were in Bethlehem, and in all the coasts thereof, from two years old and under, according to the time which he had diligently enquired of the wise men. Then was fulfilled that which was spoken by Jeremy the prophet, saying, In Rama was there a voice heard, lamentation, and weeping, and great mourning, Rachel weeping for her

children, and would not be comforted, because they are not" (Matt. 2:12-18).

"In that same hour said Jesus to the multitudes, Are ye come out as against a thief with swords and staves for to take me? I sat daily with you teaching in the temple, and ye laid no hold on me. But all this was done, that the scriptures of the prophets might be fulfilled. Then all the disciples forsook him, and fled" (Matt. 26:55-56).

"And they crucified him, and parted his garments, casting lots: that it might be fulfilled which was spoken by the prophet, They parted my garments among them, and upon my vesture did they cast lots" (Matt. 27:35).

Unfortunately, we live in a time when more children are growing up in homes without effective training for the challenges of life, and many children grow up without clear directions about their purposes in life and having less knowledge of how to go about fulfilling those purposes. Therefore, they are unprepared as adults when it comes to making the right choices.

However, God wants us to take on responsibilities as soon as we are of age, and as soon as we come to the knowledge of the truth. From the moment that we are capable of making conscious decisions, we need to take on responsibilities for taking practical steps on our own.

Make it Happen!

Take charge of the influences on your life!

Many people needlessly hold on to the excuses of having the wrong foundation for too long. We may not be able to change our pasts, but we can decide to change the future. Parents may be guilty of a person's past failures, but it does such a person no good to simply accept such a painful experience as sufficient grounds for making no further efforts towards progress now. We must all strive to move beyond painful experiences. Take responsibility for your progress, and God will help you to move forward as you do your part.

Unless we can and do take measures to curb unproductive influences from them, teachers, pastors, mentors, trainers, friends, neighbors, societies, and other strategic people in our lives are also capable of influencing our ways of thinking, as well as our priorities, enabling them to determine our progress, whether consciously or unconsciously.

We must decide to limit the negative influences on our lives and to embrace the right kind of influences on us so that we can make the greater plans of God happen!

The Bible shows that the company people keep can influence their lives, and it encourages us to resist the natural temptation to do things simply because we see the crowd or the majority of the people around us doing them. God wants us to live with a sense of sane judgment.

"He that walketh with wise men shall be wise: but a companion of fools shall be destroyed" (Prov. 13:20).

"Thou shalt not follow a multitude to do evil; neither shalt thou speak in a cause to decline after many to wrest judgment" (Ex. 23:2).

We must not follow other people blindly. We must learn to appreciate leaders but never elevate them above the word of God. The fact that a person shares something on television, even on Christian television, does not automatically make it unquestionable.

The Bible encourages us to examine the teachings that we receive.

"Prove all things; hold fast that which is good" (1 Thess. 5:21).

"And be not conformed to this world: but be ye transformed by the renewing of your mind, that ye may prove what is that good, and acceptable, and perfect, will of God" (Rom. 12:2).

The Book of Acts commends the believers in Berea because of their diligence in this. They received the word of God with openness but also took the time to search the Scriptures to be sure that they were receiving the truth of the word of God.

"These were more noble than those in Thessalonica, in that they received the word with all readiness of mind, and searched the scriptures daily, whether those things were so" (Acts 17:11).

Make it Happen!

Those that want to live above the harmful influences of other people must exalt the truth above the opinions of people, above superstitions, and above the traditions of man! Human titles are not above the word of God. Anyone who does not elevate the word of God above man's individual interpretation will be susceptible to deception and being misled.

Make up your mind to take full responsibility for what you believe; decide to make honest choices, and you will be on your way to making greater things happen in our world. Many people are living far away from the plan of God for their lives because they followed other people blindly. Achievers do not take major steps without deep personal convictions. Learn to recognize the right teachers in your life.

Let the following Bible passages inspire you to stand stronger on the word:

"O how love I thy law! it is my meditation all the day. Thou through thy commandments hast made me wiser than mine enemies: for they are ever with me. I have more understanding than all my teachers: for thy testimonies are my meditation. I understand more than the ancients, because I keep thy precepts. I have refrained my feet from every evil way, that I might keep thy word. I have not departed from thy judgments: for thou hast taught me" (Ps. 119:97–102).

"As we said before, so say I now again, If any man preach any other gospel unto you than that ye have received, let him be accursed" (Gal. 1:9).

If your present mindset is not taking you forward, be ready to examine it in the light of God's word, and if necessary, change it!

God is faithful!

God does not hold us responsible for the failures of others in our lives in those phases and moments when we had no knowledge or ability to identify such failures and make decisions of our own, but we must still move beyond such failures.

It does no one any good to keep blaming failures on growing up in a dysfunctional home, experiencing rejection from society, living under discrimination in a racist society, and so on, even when such claims are legitimate.

The failures of others may delay and disadvantage us, making progress an uphill battle that may take more effort, time, energy, and money, but we can still succeed with the help of God.

Discrimination may create an unpleasant atmosphere for progress, but you can decide to take it as a challenge and aim higher than the average person does. You can decide to hold yourself to a higher standard, study harder, work harder, behave better, learn faster, and with God on your side, you will excel!

Many foreigners are succeeding in countries other than their own. Women are succeeding in fields today that are traditionally the territories of men. Nothing and no one can stop you from succeeding and achieving the goals of God for your life if you follow the guidance of God. If you can please God, even your enemies will desire and seek to be at peace with you.

"When a man's ways please the LORD, he maketh even his enemies to be at peace with him" (Prov. 16:7).

Those that oppose you may not like the color of your skin or your gender, and they may not like your age or your style, but they will like the wealth of benefits that you can bring into their companies and the inspirations that can come to them through your life. They will find themselves desiring closer ties with you because they realize that it is in their own interest to know you better and to have you on their team! Simply make sure that you are not average.

God designed you to excel. Those who walk with their Heavenly Father never need to fail in life because of the failures of their earthly fathers.

The psalmist rightly said...

"When my father and my mother forsake me, then the LORD will take me up" (Ps. 27:10).

With God, there is hope for abandoned and forsaken children! He is the Father of the fatherless!

"A father of the fatherless, and a judge of the widows, is God in his holy habitation" (Ps. 68:5).

He promises in His word to make a way where there seems to be no way, to open doors that so that others cannot close them, and to close doors so that others will not be able to open them. God is capable of giving new beginnings to those who choose to walk with Him and uphold His name:

"Behold, I will do a new thing; now it shall spring forth; shall ye not know it? I will even make a way in the wilderness, and rivers in the desert" (Is. 43:19).

"I know thy works: behold, I have set before thee an open door, and no man can shut it: for thou hast a little strength, and hast kept my word, and hast not denied my name" (Rev. 3:8).

"Behold, I am the LORD, the God of all flesh: is there any thing too hard for me?" (Jer. 32:27).

Take charge of the influences on your life. Take responsibility for your progress, and make that mission of your dreams happen!

Assume that no one owes you progress!

Learn to live with the assumption that no one in this world owes you success. Consider it a favor when people help you or contribute positively towards your progress, and be thankful to God and to such people. Minimizing your expectations about the contributions that others are supposed to make in your life will help you to appreciate more, to achieve more, and to experience fewer disappointments in life.

Simply assume that you owe it to God, to Heaven, to your world, and to yourself to achieve all that you are capable of achieving in this world, and then step out to

Make it Happen!

accomplish the goals burning within your innermost being!

If you are an employee, assume that your employer has the obligation to pay your salary, but your financial prosperity is your own duty. You can make use of the salary to prosper.

Some people are ignorant of this fact and spend many years of their lives waiting for their employers to prosper them. They hope that promotions will come faster and that their employers will increase their salaries faster. With time, inflation increases their financial pressure, and they blame their financial hardship on their employers. The employer's responsibility is to pay salaries. Personal progress is a personal matter that is not the responsibility of an employer.

Those who take responsibility for their own progress normally invest portions of their income towards progress. They may use part of their income to finance studies next to their jobs through the Internet or by attending seminars.

Eventually they will qualify for higher levels of income. Others set some money aside to invest in a business idea that they operate next to their jobs and eventually grow it to the point where they can fire their bosses.

Progress takes dedication, and it starts with taking personal responsibility. Others work on two or more sources of income at a time because they want to speed up the realization of their financial goals, and they eventually succeed. Those who depend fully on their employers often end up progressing much slower. What must you do to move up to the next level of progress in your life? Make it happen!

Many believers talk about hearing great prophecies about their lives and receiving several confirmations of such messages, but live for many years doing nothing to fulfill them. They seem to be waiting on Heaven and on others, as if they have no responsibility to fulfill such plans. Why must God's children wait for Him to repeat His messages to them several times after they are already sure of His will for them?

While we may enjoy the reassurance of receiving confirmations, we must remember that waiting to hear them several times may be a sign of disobedience on our part. Insecurity may be natural, but we must remember that God expects us to live by faith. Living by faith necessitates that we take steps of obedience, even in challenging times.

Many believers have developed the unhealthy attitude of waiting ceaselessly for one thing or the other in the hope of having their "ideal" situation. They are often "waiting on the Lord" or "on the right timing," or they are waiting for a family member, a friend, an acquaintance, or an employer. They spend several years of their lives procrastinating and sounding spiritual about it.

We serve a God that speaks gladly and directs His children on time. He wants to see His children progress in life so that they can carry out His plans, touch lives, and glorify His name. He wants them to be faithful and active in His house and to take responsibility for their own progress.

Be Resilient

The mountain may appear too high to climb, and the journey may look too long. The "giants" may be intimidating, and your bank account may feel dry and insufficient. You may sometimes feel lonely and abandoned on the way, but you must remain strong!

God promised to be with you, even in the toughest times and moments of your life. Trust Him, and walk the talk! Live the message, and perform the commitment!

"When thou passest through the waters, I will be with thee; and through the rivers, they shall not overflow thee: when thou walkest through the fire, thou shalt not be burned; neither shall the flame kindle upon thee" (Is. 43:2).

"Fear thou not; for I am with thee: be not dismayed; for I am thy God: I will strengthen thee; yea, I will help thee; yea, I will uphold thee with the right hand of my righteousness" (Is. 41:10).

"My soul followeth hard after thee: thy right hand upholdeth me" (Ps. 63:8).

David understood the faithfulness and the power of walking with God when he declared,

"For by thee I have run through a troop; and by my God have I leaped over a wall" (Ps. 18:29).

"Blessed be the LORD my strength, which teacheth my hands to war, and my fingers to fight" (Ps. 144:1).

Discover the purpose of God for your life, and make up your mind to move forward with the mentality of an achiever. Take steps to qualify for the new level that God has in mind for you, and move forward to make it happen!

7. ARISE AND SHINE!

"Arise, shine; for thy light is come, and the glory of the LORD is risen upon thee. For, behold, the darkness shall cover the earth, and gross darkness the people: but the LORD shall arise upon thee, and his glory shall be seen upon thee. And the Gentiles shall come to thy light, and kings to the brightness of thy rising" (Is. 60:1–3).

Notice that the opening passage in this chapter begins with a call to action: *"Arise, shine...."* The passage leaves no room for passivity and procrastination. It leaves no room for excuses and personal limitations.

Let us look at the passage more closely:

1. *"Arise, shine..."***:** The word "arise" in the passage means to get up or to stand up. It means to change from a position of relaxation or inactivity into a position of readiness for action. There is a time to wait for people to give you a hand, and there is a moment when you must get up without counting on anyone's hand. This call is for you to stand up! Do not wait for anyone to give you a hand now. Use the strength that you have from God to get up!

The passage does not only call on the reader to arise. It also shows the purpose for arising. The purpose is to "shine." The word "shine" in the passage means to glow or to give out light or fire. It means to become noticeable and attractive. It means to become glorious, like becoming a star in a particular field because one excels.

"Arise, shine…" therefore means that the reader needs to get up and become a star! God wants you to shine and to bring glory to His name, and this necessitates you arising from your present level and moving up to the next level that He has for you.

Remember that God only commands us to do things when He knows that we are actually able to do them either alone or through His help. Therefore, whenever He commands, we must assume the presence of a possibility for us to carry out such commandments.

God knows that you can arise by His power and grace. Do you dare to believe Him?

> 2. *"… for thy light is come…":* Another way of saying this is "because your light has come." This is one reason why the reader must get up and shine. The word "light" in the phrase means illumination, as in clarity, brightness, understanding, inspiration, and revelation.

In other words, we are to get up and begin to shine as stars because we now have clarity, proper understanding, or revelation about the right thing to do. Proper knowledge empowers us for performance.

Make it Happen!

Ignorance keeps people down and hinders their progress.

> 3. *"... and the glory of the LORD is risen upon thee":* Notice "is risen." This means done! It is not referring to something that is about to happen, as in something to wait for, but it refers to the glory that is already on you! The children of God, walking in His will, already have this glory!

The word "glory" in the passage means the great things of God. It refers to the awesome, admirable, and special things that make God honorable and make His presence noticeable. It refers to the weighty things about Him. Weight here is not the burdensome kind of weight but the liberating type.

To understand this, imagine that you are about to go for a job interview and the president of your country calls the interviewer ahead of your appointment to ask the interviewer to strongly consider your application and to give you the job if possible. We can say that the call has weight in the sense that it is not easy for any interviewer in your country to disregard.

It has weight because of the person who made the call. The president showed you favor by throwing the weight of his office in support of your job application. The call would most likely not have the same weight if an average person, without a special and respected reputation or position, made it.

In describing your interview, we can say that the glory or reputation of the president of the country went with you into the interview room. The president's glory would be on you as you sit in the interview room. We can say that the president is behind the application or in support of the application.

In a similar way, the passage is saying that the reader needs to arise and shine because of the glory of the Lord on the reader. This is profound because the glory of the Lord on a person indicates God's weight with such a person.

Having the glory of the Lord upon you means that you have the vote of God and that you can count on His support. This already assumes that you are living a life that is pleasing to Him. It makes perfect sense for you to shine because of the glory of the Lord on you.

4. ***"For, behold, the darkness shall cover the earth, and gross darkness the people...":*** The word "darkness" in the verse means ignorance, evil, wickedness, misery, sorrow, destruction, and so on. The word "gross" in the passage means heavy, extreme, and serious.

God expects His children to shine as light in a world of ignorance, pain, sorrow, wickedness, and extreme spiritual and moral darkness. God expects us to set the standard and to show the world better examples.

We are to lead the way and model the right ways to do things. We are to be ahead of the world in spirituality, morality, science, fashion, wealth creation, justice, charity, innovations, and all other admirable areas of human endeavors.

Make it Happen!

The world at best is still ignorant, blind, and without the special revelations available to the children of the Light. However, a little light shining can be more impressive than a great light that is off.

The world appears to be shining dimly in many areas because the children of the light are sitting down passively or accepting lower standards. This is your time to change it. The world needs to see the greater thing that God left you in this world to do.

5. *"...but the LORD shall arise upon thee, and his glory shall be seen upon thee":* Notice "shall arise" and "shall be seen." You can expect these things to happen when you arise and shine, using the glory of the Lord that you already have.

In the midst of the darkness, pain, sorrow, and ignorance, here is a promise that the Lord Himself will arise over His children and cause people to see His children.

In other words, as you do your part by getting up and beginning to do all that is within your power to start shining in this dark world, God will stand with you to make His glory in your life visible.

By implication, it means that your visibility to our world depends on whether you will get up and begin to shine or not. It also means that God is waiting for you to get up and to begin to shine before your world to start experiencing the manifestation of His glory in your life. Remember that you already have a part of the glory, making it possible for you to get up and shine.

As you use that part and start shining, the Lord Himself will then stand with you and begin to do exceptional or extraordinary things through you in visible and undeniable ways. This is nothing short of God's setup to make you shine as a star in your world.

Darkness, difficulties, obstacles, opposition, and challenges cannot stop you from the manifestation that God planned for your life. You are the only one that can stop it! God wants you to be faithful with the use of the glory that you already have from Him so that He can get up in public support of your efforts and make people see His glory in you.

6. ***"And the Gentiles shall come to thy light...":*** "Gentiles" in the verse refers to a foreign nation, people, or alien. It means the people that do not know God and do not walk in covenant with Him. It refers to everyone that is foreign in knowledge or lifestyle to the principles of God. It means the heathen, or the part of the world that does not know God.

When God's children get up and begin to shine in darkness, and God stands with them to manifest His glory on them and through them, the people of the world that normally do not know God will begin to go to the light that the children of God radiate.

In other words, when the children of God begin to shine in their various ways, places, and trades, and the glory of God on His children becomes visible to the people of the world, the world will go after the light, revelation, knowledge, or inspiration coming into the dark world through the children of God.

The world goes after success, glitter, glamor, power, strength, wisdom, riches, honor, glory, inspiration, excellence, and so on. There is celebration of the people that excel in such things, and others seek to associate with and benefit from such people. The world appreciates talents and gifts and tries to take profit from associations, partnerships, and relationships with anyone who demonstrates exceptional capabilities.

Therefore, the children of God stand a better chance of influencing the world by manifesting the glory of God and shining as stars in a dark world than by being "humble" and hiding in the corners of the world, accepting lower standards, and repeating religious chants! Arise and shine!

The reality is that the world is waiting for the manifestation of the children of God.

"For the earnest expectation of the creature waiteth for the manifestation of the sons of God" (Rom. 8:19).

People like to hang around in places where things happen. Our world likes to associate with individuals and organizations that are known to make things happen. On the other hand, the ambitious world tends to disregard the worlds of those that they consider failures, and prefers to stay away from the company of the people that appear to be a bunch of losers.

Anyone who wants to influence the world must first impress the world! Your wisdom, approach, talent, gift, style, personality, love, faith, and so on needs to stand out in value to the world that God wants you to influence, and then you can expect the people in that world to come to the light that they see in you. The world needs to see and hear of you in order to come under your influence.

The Lord Jesus said…

"Ye are the light of the world. A city that is set on an hill cannot be hid. Neither do men light a candle, and put it under a bushel, but on a candlestick; and it giveth light unto all that are in the house. Let your light so shine before men, that they may see your good works, and glorify your Father which is in heaven" (Matt. 5:14–16).

God does not want His children to hide their good works and great qualities. He wants them displayed for the world to see. The light of the children of God must shine and attract people to our Heavenly Father.

7. **"… and kings to the brightness of thy rising"**: Kings here refers to royals. By implication, it means those in the highest offices and positions of influence. It refers to people in higher places, decision makers and people who command respect and determine the direction of nations, kingdoms, organizations, geographical locations, and so on.

The word "brightness" there also means "shining." In other words, royals, leaders, and decision makers in high places will pay attention to you when you rise and shine. Royals long to have access to the best talents in the land. They look for exceptional minds and rare talents.

This is why many celebrities have access to the national leaders of their countries and audiences with leaders of other countries when they travel abroad.

Royals normally operate on the highest level of excellence possible to them. They wear clothes from the best designers available. They hire the best cooks in the country. They invite top musicians to perform at their occasions. They seek counsel from the most reliable minds.

There is no room in the palace for average performance in any field or trade. The palace is not a training ground for amateurs. It is a place for those that are far above the rest. It is the place for the very best in the land.

How do they know the best in the land? It is quite simple. They seek those that are already shining. Royals send out scouts or talent hunters to search for the unique breeds of people that are worthy of palace quality.

People with secret talents do not receive invitations to perform in the palace. To stand a chance of receiving an invitation to the palace, one must first shine noticeably. The gift or talent must already be visible for others to see.

We cannot hide our potential and still influence nations. We must first impress our world if we want to influence our world. We must first shine where we are if we want to have audiences in higher places.

The Bible says...

"A man's gift maketh room for him, and bringeth him before great men" (Prov. 18:16).

Primarily, the word "gift" in the verse also means a present or a reward. It is that which brings benefits or pleasure to the receiver. In the most practical sense, it refers to that which we give to someone in the form of a present, such as gold, silver, an artifact, merchandise, and so on. They are often things that we leave behind for the receivers.

However, by extension, a gift may also be a presentation that leaves an impression behind. A heart-touching performance that keeps a person happy for several days is also a gift. A faithful servant is also a gift. Talented people are gifts to their churches, neighborhoods, cities, nations, and, sometimes, to the entire world.

That which you are able to give to your world is your gift to your world. The talents, skills, experiences, and all of the natural and supernatural resources and potential in your life can help you to make positive contributions to your world.

As you begin to use them in the spirit of commitment, faithfulness, and excellence, greater doors will open, and you will become more attractive to those people who value and appreciate excellence. Eventually you will be the kind of person that royals long to be associated with, the kind of person that scouts and talent-hunters in higher places are searching the land to find.

Our world is constantly looking for something better, stronger, more impressive, more useful, more profitable, more entertaining, more convenient, and so on. You may be walking around with the next multimillion-dollar innovative business idea that will make life easier for people, create new jobs, strengthen relationships, and change the status quo for thousands and possibly millions of people around the world.

You may be an inventor with one or more solutions to challenges hindering the efficiencies of one or more industries. You may hold the cure to a disease plaguing the world. You may have within you the songs that will heal the emotional wounds of millions of people around the world. Only God knows all that you are capable of doing for your world.

Try to imagine the number of lives that you can touch if you will arise and shine! Try to think about the differences that you can make if you will step up to the next level and allow your world to see that star that God designed you to be. God has great gifts in you, and you are His great gift to your world. Our world is waiting to benefit from all that you have to offer.

Recognizing Your Moments of Destiny

There is a time and a season for everything on the earth, and true achievers know how to recognize and seize their moments.

The Bible declares,

"To every thing there is a season, and a time to every purpose under the heaven" (Eccl. 3:1).

Recognizing the times and the seasons of your life and the purpose of God for them will help you to make the best use of the opportunities of your life. Many people do not understand seasons and do not know the right things at the right time.

Moments of destiny are those special moments or experiences that position you to recognize signs or to identify feelings or people that are crucial to the fulfillment of your destiny. They are moments that wake you up from your sleep, literally and figuratively, and then confront you with your destiny.

They make you think and help you to see things that are necessary for you to make mission-critical decisions for your progress in the will of God for you. Such moments open your eyes to see points and help your mind to focus on a few things that are important for your empowerment and advancement.

It is a moment when you meet a person and feel that such a meeting is not by accident or coincidence. It is that moment when an idea comes into your mind and arrests you deep within, and you feel that you need to do something about it. That is when you suddenly feel uncomfortable with your "success," and you sense a pull within you to reach for higher goals.

It is the moments that you hear people in your world praising you for your great accomplishment, but you then hear a voice within you telling you that you are still far away from reaching your potential. Your moment of destiny will provoke you for higher accomplishments, help you to see the greater things ahead, and rebuke you when unhealthy pride knocks at your door.

To shine, you must understand your moments of destiny and make proper use of them. Let us turn to the Bible for a few inspirations and examples to help us understand moments of destiny better.

> **1. When the vision begins to speak:** God's vision for our lives "speaks" at the appropriate times. As we have seen earlier in this chapter, whenever God wants to take people higher, they begin to feel a sense of dissatisfaction with their levels. They will be thinking about greater things and higher goals. This is because God is working within them to move them forward in His plans.

"For the vision is yet for an appointed time, but at the end it shall speak, and not lie: though it tarry, wait for it; because it will surely come, it will not tarry. Behold, his soul which is lifted up is not upright in him: but the just shall live by his faith" (Hab. 2:3–4).

Once the vision starts speaking, we must be strong in God and stand ready to act by faith. Faith is confidence in God—the kind of confidence that makes us take the steps necessary to fulfill His purpose in our lives.

You hear the vision "speak" when suddenly God reminds you of the dreams of greatness that you had several years ago. The vision speaks when you suddenly start seeing images of divine assignment that you forgot a long time ago. At that moment, you must make up your mind to pursue that purpose.

Jacob had a dream in Bethel while running away from his brother, Esau. He then prayed to God and asked God for protection and prosperity, vowing to give tithes to God and to build God a house in Bethel if God would protect him and bring him back there safely.

"And Jacob rose up early in the morning, and took the stone that he had put for his pillows, and set it up for a pillar, and poured oil upon the top of it. And he called the name of that place Bethel: but the name of that city was called Luz at the first. And Jacob vowed a vow, saying, If God will be with me, and will keep me in this way that I go, and will give me bread to eat, and raiment to put on, So that I come again to my father's house in peace; then shall the LORD be my God: And this stone, which I have set for a pillar, shall be God's house: and of all that thou shalt give me I will surely give the tenth unto thee" (Gen. 28:18-22).

As most Bible students know, God did protect and prosper Jacob. Jacob ended up in the house of Laban, where he served the cunning man for several years, endured cheating, and eventually prospered through the help of God.

As he tried to settle down there, God asked him to move away from Laban and head in the direction of his vision:

"I am the God of Bethel, where thou anointedst the pillar, and where thou vowedst a vow unto me: now arise, get thee out from this land, and return unto the land of thy kindred" (Gen. 31:13).

Jacob left Laban in obedience to God, met and reconciled with his brother Esau along the way, and tried to settle down without going all the way to Bethel. He was a successful man at this point in his life, and he simply wanted to settle down with his family and enjoy some peace after so many years of running away from his brother and going through hardship in the house of Laban.

However, God still wanted him to pursue the vision of building a place of worship in Bethel. The vision of Bethel then began to speak to him! God confronted Jacob with one of his moments of destiny and asked Jacob to move on to Bethel.

Here is the passage:

"And God said unto Jacob, Arise, go up to Bethel, and dwell there: and make there an altar unto God, that appeared unto thee when thou fleddest from the face of Esau thy brother. Then Jacob said unto his household, and to all that were with him, Put away the strange gods that are among you, and be clean, and change your garments: And let us arise, and go up to Bethel; and I will make there an altar unto God, who answered me in the day of my distress, and was with me in the way which I went" (Gen. 35:1–3).

Whenever the vision speaks back to you, see it as one of your moments of destiny, and make the necessary decisions to follow the direction of such a moment.

2. ***When you are Jacob and give birth to Joseph:*** Jacob was in charge of Laban's animals. Bible students know that Laban grew in wealth for several years because of the hand of God on Jacob. However, Laban, who was also his father-in-law, was neither grateful nor generous towards Jacob.

Jacob tolerated injustice from his father-in-law and endured living and working with him for several years, but all of that changed after the birth of Joseph!

"And it came to pass, when Rachel had born Joseph, that Jacob said unto Laban, Send me away, that I may go unto mine own place, and to my country. Give me my wives and my children, for whom I have served thee, and let me go: for thou knowest my service which I have done thee" (Gen. 30:25–26).

The birth of Joseph made Jacob realize that his family was growing larger without resources in place to secure a bright future for them. He realized that his responsibility was growing without security for the future.

He was getting older, without anything to call his own, and clearly without any inheritance to leave for his children. He then decided to move forward with his life and to secure a better and brighter future for his offspring.

Make it Happen!

Laban realized that he was about to lose a reliable worker and began to negotiate for Jacob to stay.

"And Laban said unto him, I pray thee, if I have found favour in thine eyes, tarry: for I have learned by experience that the LORD hath blessed me for thy sake. And he said, Appoint me thy wages, and I will give it. And he said unto him, Thou knowest how I have served thee, and how thy cattle was with me" (Gen. 30:27–29).

The negotiation resulted in an agreement that finally made Jacob wealthy.

The birth of Joseph was a major moment of destiny for Jacob. He felt the pressure of the moment and decided that he could no longer continue to live a lifestyle that was not securing the future of his children. He decided to go with the feeling of the moment, and the result was a life-transforming deal that made him the envy of the children of Laban. He decided to arise and do something to change the future of his children. God blessed him to shine, but he was living like a loser! He could no longer accept the status quo, and he decided to talk to Laban about it. His life was never the same after that experience. His days of lack were over—forever!

The "birth-of-Joseph" moment of destiny comes in the form of an event or a specific experience. It is the wake-up call that people receive when they have exceptional experiences. Some people get this experience after miraculously surviving a serious illness or a major accident. Others experience this after going through humiliation or suffering injustice.

Some people get this experience after losing a job and realizing that they have no pension plan in place. Still others get this experience after becoming a year older and realizing that they are growing older too fast and feeling unaccomplished!

Some experience this after losing someone that is precious to them. Others experience it after a sudden humbling breakthrough. Some experience this after receiving a letter from a creditor. Others experience it after going through betrayal in the hands of someone that they trusted.

The Prodigal Son in the Bible also had such a moment. This son, eager to have independence from the family, took his inheritance while his father was still living. He then traveled to a far country, where he enjoyed his life daily, wasted his money living carelessly, and ended up broke.

To make matters worse, the land began to experience famine. This young man from a wealthy home soon found himself with a job taking care of swine. His situation deteriorated, and in his hunger, he began to develop an appetite for the feed of the pigs! This was his wake-up moment with destiny! He came to self-realization, and his life changed from that moment.

Here is how the Bible describes his experience and the turning point:

"And he said, A certain man had two sons: And the younger of them said to his father, Father, give me the portion of goods that falleth to me. And he divided unto them his living. And not many days after the younger son

gathered all together, and took his journey into a far country, and there wasted his substance with riotous living. And when he had spent all, there arose a mighty famine in that land; and he began to be in want. And he went and joined himself to a citizen of that country; and he sent him into his fields to feed swine. And he would fain have filled his belly with the husks that the swine did eat: and no man gave unto him. And when he came to himself, he said, How many hired servants of my father's have bread enough and to spare, and I perish with hunger!" (Luke 15:11–17).

The desire to eat swine food made him think about his father's house. He realized that the servants in his father's house had food to eat and enough to spare. He decided that he would rather be a servant in the house of his father than remain in his present situation. He made up his mind to return home and apply for a job with his father as a hired servant.

"I will arise and go to my father, and will say unto him, Father, I have sinned against heaven, and before thee, And am no more worthy to be called thy son: make me as one of thy hired servants" (Luke 15:18–19).

He then started the journey back home. Those familiar with the story know that his father ended up accepting him back as a son with elaborate celebration!

The Prodigal Son seized a moment of destiny, and it changed his predicament.

Learn to recognize your moments of destiny and take appropriate steps. Many people miss their opportunities with destiny because they do not learn how to recognize their moments of destiny. Be one of the relatively few people who recognize their moments and make the best use of them.

   3. **When divine providence finds you:** Divine providence is the hand of God guiding human affairs to favor His will for a person or a people. It is one of the many ways that God indicates His presence in the life of a person or a people.

In general, God leaves man in charge of the affairs of this world. However, God reserves the discretion to intervene occasionally to create conditions necessary for the establishment of His purpose. He then lets man see His hand in the form of actions that point to God's intervention.

The actions can manifest in the form of a special favor, a miracle, a special experience, and so on. Divine providence can manifest in the form of opened doors, closed doors, supernatural provisions or supplies, and exceptional contacts and strategic relationships.

Divine providence is a moment of destiny indicating the determination of God to work things out in favor of His child, or His people, to further the purpose of destiny for the glory of His name.

Divine providence is a "green light" from Heaven for one to proceed with confidence in God. It is God's way of providing the chance, connection, supplies, experience, approval, and other things and factors necessary to boost confidence and reassurance in His children for the execution of His purpose. They are the *signs* and the *wonders* that God shows to favor His plans.

It is in that place and that time when God has things in place for your success and gives you a tangible sign to confirm His support for you. It is one of those moments when having faith is easy because you can see the hand of God and feel His commitment. It is that time when things look too good to be true and you cannot explain why you deserve such an experience.

It is that moment when you are wondering how long the great thing you are experiencing will last. Divine providence makes you feel that you are on Heaven's agenda and that God is giving you special advantages.

It is that moment when you receive special wisdom and knowledge from Heaven about the way out of a situation that you had no prior experience to handle. It is that moment when your opinion amazes you, in addition to amazing your audience, because it is higher than the level of anything that you have heard before.

Divine providence is God arising to your defense and exposing the false accusations of your opponents. Divine providence is God answering your prayers, even before you are finished praying, and even giving you additional things beyond your request.

The Lord declared in the book of Isaiah:

"And it shall come to pass, that before they call, I will answer; and while they are yet speaking, I will hear" (Is. 65:24).

David understood this when he wrote,

"The king shall joy in thy strength, O LORD; and in thy salvation how greatly shall he rejoice! Thou hast given him his heart's desire, and hast not withholden the request of his lips. Selah. For thou preventest him with the blessings of goodness: thou settest a crown of pure gold on his head. He asked life of thee, and thou gavest it him, even length of days for ever and ever. His glory is great in thy salvation: honour and majesty hast thou laid upon him" (Ps. 21:1-5).

"The LORD is the portion of mine inheritance and of my cup: thou maintainest my lot. The lines are fallen unto me in pleasant places; yea, I have a goodly heritage" (Ps. 16:5-6).

Divine providence is God watching over His faithful children and taking care of them in times of special needs:

"Thou shalt tread upon the lion and adder: the young lion and the dragon shalt thou trample under feet. Because he hath set his love upon me, therefore will I deliver him: I will set him on high, because he hath known my name. He shall call upon me, and I will answer him: I will be with him in trouble; I will deliver him, and honour him. With long life will I satisfy him, and shew him my salvation" (Ps. 91:13-16).

"Remember ye not the former things, neither consider the things of old. Behold, I will do a new thing; now it shall spring forth; shall ye not know it? I will even make a way in the wilderness, and rivers in the desert" (Is. 43:18-19).

Make it Happen!

Divine providence can lead to a life-changing personal spiritual experience, as was the case of Saul.

The children of Israel wanted a king. Saul was looking for the lost asses of his father. By what appeared to be a coincidence, he met Samuel, the prophet, and heard that he was God's choice to be king over the land. Samuel anointed him and then sent him back home, with specific instructions about some experiences to expect on the way back home.

Samuel told Saul:

"And let it be, when these signs are come unto thee, that thou do as occasion serve thee; for God is with thee" (1 Sam. 10:7).

Notice that Samuel instructed him to do as occasion served him. We shall look at this shortly, but first, let us read more about his experiences.

As Saul left Samuel, the Bible tells us that Saul became a different person:

"And when they came thither to the hill, behold, a company of prophets met him; and the Spirit of God came upon him, and he prophesied among them. And it came to pass, when all that knew him beforetime saw that, behold, he prophesied among the prophets, then the people said one to another, What is this that is come unto the son of Kish? Is Saul also among the prophets?" (1 Sam. 10:10–11).

The change in the life of Saul was evident to the people who saw him. Encounters with God often result in visible transformation of lives.

Samuel then called the people together and anointed Saul king over the children of Israel. He sent the people home after that, but God allowed a group of people to follow him. Whenever God sets people up to shine, He also touches the hearts of others to stand with them and to follow them for the establishment of the purpose of God. People hardly rise to shine alone.

"And Saul also went home to Gibeah; and there went with him a band of men, whose hearts God had touched" (1 Sam. 10:26).

Saul was in touch with his destiny. He did not only have followers. He also had jesters—those that did not receive him in the capacity of the hand of God on his life. These people rejected him, yet he remained calm. Those who must rise and shine must also prepare to handle opposition. Do not expect the entire world to celebrate you when you meet your moment of destiny.

"But the children of Belial said, How shall this man save us? And they despised him, and brought him no presents. But he held his peace" (1 Sam. 10:27).

Shortly after this, there was another moment of destiny in the life of King Saul. Nahash the Ammonite camped around Jabeshgilead, part of the territory of Israel, and threatened the people with war. The people of Jabeshgilead suggested serving the Ammonites in exchange for peace, but the enemy refused their offer and came up with a ridiculous counteroffer:

Make it Happen!

"Then Nahash the Ammonite came up, and encamped against Jabeshgilead: and all the men of Jabesh said unto Nahash, Make a covenant with us, and we will serve thee. And Nahash the Ammonite answered them, On this condition will I make a covenant with you, that I may thrust out all your right eyes, and lay it for a reproach upon all Israel" (1 Sam. 11:1–2).

The elders of Jabeshgilead then sent out messengers to the rest of the children of Israel describing their predicament and asking for help. Unfortunately, the rest of the land only showed sympathy without offering the military support that they desperately needed in the situation. The messengers also reached the place of Saul, but he was out of town taking care of his father's herd at the time.

Although he was already the king, he continued with his usual life, doing nothing in the direction of the plan of God for making him king, and God was about to change that for good!

"Then came the messengers to Gibeah of Saul, and told the tidings in the ears of the people: and all the people lifted up their voices, and wept" (1 Sam. 11:4).

Simply weeping does not resolve some challenges, especially those that are military in nature. Sympathy and empathy may indicate true love, but they are not sufficient in solving practical challenges. People need real solutions when they have serious problems.

While the rest of the children of Israel cried helplessly, Saul arrived at what was to be another major moment of destiny for him.

Let us read to see how God used the situation to deliver the people, make King Saul shine, and get him back on track in the will of God for his life:

"And, behold, Saul came after the herd out of the field; and Saul said, What aileth the people that they weep? And they told him the tidings of the men of Jabesh. And the Spirit of God came upon Saul when he heard those tidings, and his anger was kindled greatly" (1 Sam. 11:5-6).

Notice the deep inner anger that he felt after hearing about the situation. The Bible shows that the anger boiled in him because the Spirit of God came on him. This inner stirring by God was part of his moment with destiny. The situation was part of the divine providence for the manifestation of Saul; it gave God the opportunity to let Saul begin to live up to his anointing as king.

With the anger deep within Saul, he took the initiative to send messengers to the rest of the land of Israel, calling on recruits to go into battle and deliver the people of Jabeshgilead.

Here is the result:

"And he took a yoke of oxen, and hewed them in pieces, and sent them throughout all the coasts of Israel by the hands of messengers, saying, Whosoever cometh not forth after Saul and after Samuel, so shall it be done

unto his oxen. And the fear of the LORD fell on the people, and they came out with one consent. And when he numbered them in Bezek, the children of Israel were three hundred thousand, and the men of Judah thirty thousand. And they said unto the messengers that came, Thus shall ye say unto the men of Jabeshgilead, To morrow, by that time the sun be hot, ye shall have help. And the messengers came and shewed it to the men of Jabesh; and they were glad" (1 Sam. 11:7-9).

Saul experienced divine providence and acted as occasion served him, and the men of war responded to his call. As a result, he was able to make the sad people of Jabeshgilead glad with hope for deliverance. His army defeated the enemy, and the entire land was glad!

God used the situation to demonstrate His power through King Saul, and he became an instant celebrity in the land. They stood in his support and made a stand to defeat all opposition against his position in the land:

"And the people said unto Samuel, Who is he that said, Shall Saul reign over us? bring the men, that we may put them to death. And Saul said, There shall not a man be put to death this day: for to day the LORD hath wrought salvation in Israel" (1 Sam. 11:12-13).

The people were aware earlier of opposition against King Saul in the land but did nothing to stop the troublemakers. Saul had yet to win their respect and admiration. He had yet to win their battle. He had yet to shine in the land. Therefore, they did not fight for him. With the victory over the Ammonite, he proved that he was above the rest, and the people instantly noticed his manifestation and were willing to kill for him!

It is worth noticing that he forgave those that opposed him and directed the attention of the land to the Lord, preferring to celebrate the Lord's victory.

People prefer to rally around leaders that fight for them. Saul needed an opportunity to shine, and the challenge at hand provided the perfect chance!

Divine providence may come with some challenges, but you need to recognize the hand of God in the difficulties and act appropriately for the occasion. You need to follow the pull that you feel deep within and stand up for the needs around you, and you will experience divine support.

Remember that it is easier to see stars at night. The light shines brighter in darkness. Tackle challenges and shine! Run into the battle if you feel the pull to do so. Stand up for action when others are only crying helplessly. Face that difficult situation, and take that difficult step!

Some of the most successful people throughout history are those that solved problems in their societies. They took on challenges, looked for solutions, found solutions, and earned the respect of humanity. Dare to take on challenges when you see the "green light" from Heaven. Learn to identify the hand of God in tough times.

God uses difficulties to work towards the manifestation of His children. Great achievers know that most adversities come with opportunities. Pay attention to the needs of others, take steps to make a difference in your world with the opportunities that you have, and you will shine!

Once you conclude that God is on your side, do as occasion serves you. This simply means doing the right thing according to the need of the situation. Use your God-guided discretion.

Set yourself up for your world to discover you.

Visibility is more crucial than ability when it comes to shining in your world. What you are able to do only gets the attention of the world when someone out there knows that you are capable of doing it.

Ability is what you can do. Visibility is what people see that you can do. Therefore, being in a position for people to discover your abilities is crucial if you want to shine in your world.

A flashlight only makes a difference in darkness when you switch the power to the "ON" position and it actually gives light to those in darkness. That is when it becomes useful. Until then, it only has the potential to give light. The world does not celebrate potential. Our world celebrates accomplishment, or the perception of it. People celebrate those who achieve greatness or those that they perceive or believe to have achieved greatness.

The "fastest man on the planet" is not necessarily the fastest man in the world. He is just the fastest of all of the men in the world that took part in the race or contest responsible for such a title. In other words, a young man in a remote place that did not participate in such a contest but has the ability to run faster will not be the "fastest man on the planet."

The young man's failure to participate in the contest may be because he never heard about the race, because he did not believe that he stood a chance, or because he did not want to be famous, and so on. Great titles do not necessarily go to the best people in the world. They go to winners. Winners are simply the best among participants.

Your ability to run a great company will not count until you actually run one. Your ability to write a great book will only begin to count when you write one. That great song burning inside of you will only get attention when you get it out. Your ability to invent the next solution to a problem in your world will only matter when you carry out the invention and position it for your world to see. No one will know you as a great speaker if you only speak to yourself in front of the mirror.

To shine, you must position yourself for discovery in your field. Someone must begin to see that you are special. That person will then tell the next person. The new person will become curious to see what you are able to do, and you will soon have two people paying attention to you.

If you continue to perform remarkably, these people will speak to others, and the others to others. In time, the word will be out there about your abilities, prompting those that are likely to benefit from such abilities to look for you, increasing your audience, and deepening your reach. In time, you will touch more lives with your ability.

Your world needs to know about your capabilities. God may set you up and expose these capabilities. Some loved ones around you may discover them and begin to promote you. However, you may also take steps to help your world discover you. This requires being proactive on your part.

Let us now see a few things that you can do to make it easier for your world to discover you:

1. ***Behave yourself!*** Those that know you will notice your character faster than they notice your gifts. Excellence in character leads to attraction and favor. Therefore, you must learn to behave yourself.

People are watching you even when you are not aware that they are. The favor of God on your life will translate into an enduring favor with reasonable people when you behave yourself!

Most Bible students know that David had the favor of God on his life as a young man. However, a careful study of his life would reveal that he behaved himself wisely at all times as a young man:

"And David went out whithersoever Saul sent him, and behaved himself wisely: and Saul set him over the men of

war, and he was accepted in the sight of all the people, and also in the sight of Saul's servants" (1 Sam. 18:5)

"And David behaved himself wisely in all his ways; and the LORD was with him. Wherefore when Saul saw that he behaved himself very wisely, he was afraid of him" (1 Sam. 18:14–15).

"Then the princes of the Philistines went forth: and it came to pass, after they went forth, that David behaved himself more wisely than all the servants of Saul; so that his name was much set by" (1 Sam. 18:30).

David was young, but he behaved in character, with skills, and in line with the principles and rules of war, resulting in excellent performance on the battlefield, and thereby commanding respect from the crowd and from the elites of his time.

Favor dwells with commitment, faithfulness, integrity, proper character, and excellence. Grace and favor come from God, but character depends on man.

Paul instructed Timothy to be an example:

"Let no man despise thy youth; but be thou an example of the believers, in word, in conversation, in charity, in spirit, in faith, in purity" (1 Tim. 4:12).

Paul wanted Timothy to be an example to all believers. Be the better example to others in the values that you uphold.

Develop excellent character behind the scenes, and you will excel in public. When you are real in private, you will not need to pretend in public. Many people understand the importance of character and try to impress their world in the public without the deep moral and spiritual depth resulting from a consistent real commitment to character in their personal, private lives. The result is an unsustainable show of integrity that will become known in a matter of time.

Such people profess faithfulness on the outside while they are unfaithful behind the scenes. They behave friendly on the outside, but act contrary to the principles of true friendliness in secret. They vote their support for leadership on the outside but speak against the same leaders behind the scenes. They pretend to be more than they are and do not stand the test of time.

The Lord Jesus Christ refers to people with such double standards and pretentious lifestyles as "hypocrites":

"Woe unto you, scribes and Pharisees, hypocrites! for ye make clean the outside of the cup and of the platter, but within they are full of extortion and excess. Thou blind Pharisee, cleanse first that which is within the cup and platter, that the outside of them may be clean also. Woe unto you, scribes and Pharisees, hypocrites! for ye are like unto whited sepulchres, which indeed appear beautiful outward, but are within full of dead men's bones, and of all uncleanness" (Matt. 23:25–27).

Be what you believe, and live what you preach! Live the values that you uphold, even when no one is watching you, and you will live the same values in front of people effortlessly. Reality in seclusion will flow in public more naturally.

Hypocrisy eventually leads to embarrassment:

"For there is nothing covered, that shall not be revealed; neither hid, that shall not be known. Therefore whatsoever ye have spoken in darkness shall be heard in the light; and that which ye have spoken in the ear in closets shall be proclaimed upon the housetops" (Luke 12:2-3).

Excellence in character will make your world notice you. Behaving yourself will have a positive impact on how your world perceives you.

"Even a fool, when he holdeth his peace, is counted wise: and he that shutteth his lips is esteemed a man of understanding" (Prov. 17:28).

"Let not mercy and truth forsake thee: bind them about thy neck; write them upon the table of thine heart: So shalt thou find favour and good understanding in the sight of God and man" (Prov. 3:3-4).

Speaking of the Lord Jesus Christ, the Bible says…

"And Jesus increased in wisdom and stature, and in favour with God and man" (Luke 2:52).

Care about people sincerely, and it will show with time. Love truly. Serve honestly. Believe genuinely.

In the Bible, Daniel first stood out for his excellent character:

Make it Happen!

"Forasmuch as an excellent spirit, and knowledge, and understanding, interpreting of dreams, and shewing of hard sentences, and dissolving of doubts, were found in the same Daniel, whom the king named Belteshazzar: now let Daniel be called, and he will shew the interpretation" (Dan. 5:12).

"I have even heard of thee, that the spirit of the gods is in thee, and that light and understanding and excellent wisdom is found in thee" (Dan. 5:14)

"Then this Daniel was preferred above the presidents and princes, because an excellent spirit was in him; and the king thought to set him over the whole realm" (Dan. 6:3)

Daniel was exceptional in character, and the world around him noticed it. Eventually the king heard about him, and it paved the way for him to shine in a foreign country.

His progress was not without challenges. Some of his colleagues were jealous of his progress and tried to hinder him. They looked at him critically to see how to bring him down, but Daniel was solid! He was real, and they could not find legitimate reasons to raise allegations against him; therefore, they had to devise dubious ways to obstruct him.

"Then the presidents and princes sought to find occasion against Daniel concerning the kingdom; but they could find none occasion nor fault; forasmuch as he was faithful, neither was there any error or fault found in him. Then said these men, We shall not find any occasion

against this Daniel, except we find it against him concerning the law of his God" (Dan. 6:4–5).

They came up with a law designed to get him in trouble, but he remained faithful to God, and God protected him. His opponents ended up in trouble! Their obstacles only helped him to climb up higher and to shine brighter, bringing glory to God.

"So this Daniel prospered in the reign of Darius, and in the reign of Cyrus the Persian" (Dan. 6:28).

Some readers may say, "Well, I am not Daniel, and I am certainly not perfect in all of my ways. How can I follow this principle?" The answer is simple. Start where you are, being real with God and with your conscience in private, and being your best in front of people, and continue to grow. People will notice your sincerity, even if you make mistakes.

Your world does not necessarily expect you to be perfect in all areas of life. People just expect you to be real and to be a good example to them in the values that matter most to them.

2. **Grow in your gifts and talents:** God gives gifts, but we must develop skills and excel in talents in order to grow and stand out. Your personal effort is essential in growing your gifts. Practice, train, and be critical of your level so that you can strive higher and get better at the things that you do. Do not settle for the applause of people. Do not settle for being the champion of the little community that you live

Make it Happen!

in. Grow beyond your current level, and people will start recommending you for the next one.

If you are a speaker, speak your best in the little meetings until people begin to feel that the city needs to hear you. Then speak your best in that city meeting until people begin to feel that the nation needs to hear you.

Speak your best at the national meeting until people begin to feel that the world needs to hear you. Earn the next level of platform in the hearts and minds of those that you serve now, and you will end up on the ultimate platform with time.

Do not settle for the place where you are unless you are sure that God has nothing higher for you. Grow by listening to your critics as well as to those that praise you. If you have no critics, then become your own critic. Learn to constantly and consistently improve on the things that you do best.

If you can bake cakes, back that skill with excellence and people will talk about it. In a matter of time, someone may ask you to bake a cake for her wedding. Use the chance to bake your best, and someone at the wedding may fall in love with your cake and seek contact with you. With time, the word may go around, and you will become a celebrity cake baker once you learn to package and price your services appropriately for your target market.

Therefore, whatever your gifts are, grow them and grow in them. Do not underestimate any opportunity. Someone is watching you, and that person knows somebody that knows someone else that knows another person that has been praying and hoping to meet a person like you.

People naturally speak about the people and the things that impress them. Do not wait for bigger or better platforms before you do your best. Be your best, and give your best, now! Use your present opportunities to excel in performance, just where you are now, and you will stand out taller and shine brighter, making it easier for better platforms to notice and find you!

Being your best where you are will prepare the way for you to gain access to the places in need of your qualities.

The Lord Jesus Christ spent quality time with a Samaritan woman, and that opened the door for Him to reach several people because she broadcasted her experience with Him:

"The woman then left her waterpot, and went her way into the city, and saith to the men, Come, see a man, which told me all things that ever I did: is not this the Christ? Then they went out of the city, and came unto him" (John 4:28–30).

The Lord touched just one woman, and she broadcasted her experience to her people. As a result, several people from her city went to Him, and they were able to experience Him in person.

"And many of the Samaritans of that city believed on him for the saying of the woman, which testified, He told me all that ever I did. So when the Samaritans were

come unto him, they besought him that he would tarry with them: and he abode there two days. And many more believed because of his own word; And said unto the woman, Now we believe, not because of thy saying: for we have heard him ourselves, and know that this is indeed the Christ, the Saviour of the world" (John 4:39–42).

Do not underestimate your current customer, client, or audience. Strive to leave everyone that you meet with a lasting impression. Shine now!

Learn and improve constantly and consistently. If necessary, take courses, attend seminars, read books, ask questions, attend training sessions, and do whatever it takes to improve on your current level. Do not settle for anything less than all that God wants for you. Grow and shine!

3. ***Look for opportunities to serve with your expertise:*** To be great and to achieve extraordinary accomplishments, you must have the courage to think big, the confidence to act boldly, and the humility to serve others.

The Lord Jesus said,

"But it shall not be so among you: but whosoever will be great among you, let him be your minister; And whosoever will be chief among you, let him be your servant" (Matt. 20:26–27).

Use your gift to build someone around you. Let your environment benefit from the precious qualities in your life. Serving is part of giving. Serve gladly.

The Bible tells us,

"Even so ye, forasmuch as ye are zealous of spiritual gifts, seek that ye may excel to the edifying of the church" (1 Cor. 14:12).

Volunteer in the family, in the church, in your community, and in your world. Do not worry if others simply use you. Those that do not want others to use them often end up becoming useless in their society and, with time, become useless in their world.

Learn to guard against abuse, but do not let the fear of abuse prevent you from being useful. To suffer abuse means to go through mistreatment, unjust exploitation, and manipulation or intimidation.

Serve in an orderly manner, and respect all applicable rules and people in their right places, but do not sit back and live idly in a world full of needs.

Serving can make others use you without them abusing you. If you run a business, pay special attention to service, and your business will shine.

Now is the best time!

What are you waiting for? Now is the best time to do the right thing. Remember that today used to be "tomorrow." Do not live like a procrastinator. Take actions today to make tomorrow better. You cannot change your past, but you can influence tomorrow by the decisions that you make today. Start now!

Make it Happen!

God encourages procrastination and encourages critical actions in the now!

"(For he saith, I have heard thee in a time accepted, and in the day of salvation have I succoured thee: behold, now is the accepted time; behold, now is the day of salvation.)" (2 Cor. 6:2).

"While it is said, To day if ye will hear his voice, harden not your hearts, as in the provocation" (Heb. 3:15).

"Say not ye, There are yet four months, and then cometh harvest? behold, I say unto you, Lift up your eyes, and look on the fields; for they are white already to harvest" (John 4:35).

Begin to surround your life with the right people now. Start working on that business plan now. Enroll in that online course now! Start setting money aside towards your financial goal now! Review your priorities now. Defeat those bad habits, and adopt new healthy habits now!

God is waiting for you to arise, shine, and make it happen! You owe it to yourself, to Heaven, and to your world to live up to your full potential. Your time is here!

"Arise, shine; for thy light is come, and the glory of the LORD is risen upon thee. For, behold, the darkness shall cover the earth, and gross darkness the people: but the LORD shall arise upon thee, and his glory shall be seen upon thee. And the Gentiles shall come to thy light, and kings to the brightness of thy rising" (Is. 60:1–3)

Make it happen!

About the Author

Emmanuel Idu had a life-changing spiritual encounter in his teenage years and began public speaking at an early age. He has a strong apostolic voice and a respectable insight into the Bible, allowing him to communicate deep biblical principles in clear and simple language.

Apostle Idu speaks to a wide range of audiences at strategic events worldwide and serves as the Bishop and General Overseer of a growing number of churches.

Emmanuel is a gifted strategist, course developer, speaker, writer, and progress trainer. His unconventional mind has distinguished him as a personal confidant to many leaders around the world.

He is happily married to Irene, and they have two daughters, Caroline and Darielle.

www.ingramcontent.com/pod-product-compliance
Lightning Source LLC
LaVergne TN
LVHW051832080426
835512LV00018B/2835